# The 100 Greatest Track & Field Battles of the Twentieth Century

by J. Hollobaugh

THE 100 GREATEST TRACK & FIELD BATTLES OF THE
TWENTIETH CENTURY

Copyright © 2012 Michtrack Books.
3130 Kensington * Dexter, Michigan 48130
michtrack@aol.com


ISBN-13:
978-1470149314

ISBN-10:
1470149311

**Cover photo:** Billy Mills outsprinting the field to capture the 1964
Olympic gold medal in the 10,000m run. [*History Division, United
States Marine Corps; public domain*]

**Back cover:** clippings from *Waycross Journal-Herald*, May 17,
1971; *The Bulletin*, October 14, 1964; and *Gettysburg Times*,
December 22, 1954.

# INTRODUCTION

The genesis of this book came in 1999 when I was writing a weekly online track column for ESPN.com. The joy of such a column is obvious: the opportunity to write about track and field all the time. The burden was equally obvious: having to write about track & field virtually all the time. Not really so bad usually, but there were inevitably slow news weeks, or weeks where true athletic accomplishment was overshadowed by the negatives of drug stories, money stories, or whining superstars stories.

I first fell in love with track and field by thumbing through the pages of old copies of *Track & Field News*. These were thrilling issues, filled with the exploits of John Walker, Filbert Bayi, and Steve Prefontaine. I so wanted to travel back in time and be at those races and absorb the rarified atmosphere of that kind of greatness firsthand. Perhaps that's what stimulated my interest in track history. Even if I wasn't present--or even alive then--I didn't want to forget those magic moments. I wanted to share them. In the end, for me and for many track fans, it's all about the love of a great battle on the track or the field.

But what defines a great competition? I once knew a noted track expert who felt disgusted if he traveled to an Olympics or World Championships, saw some of the best runners of the world on the track, and had to watch them run a tactical race instead of chase after the world record. For him, a great race was a fast race, period.

Honestly, though, after seeing my fair share of world records in person, I came to the realization that the excitement often came from swiveling my eyes back and forth from the runners to the stadium clock, wondering if they could produce the magic numbers. While that's certainly a legitimate form of excitement, I had to admit that if we turned off all the clocks, what we would be watching at many Grand Prix meets is a fairly boring exhibition of a runner pushing the edge of the envelope figuratively holding the hand of a hired pacemaker.

That's when I generated my own definition of a great race: a race that would be fun to watch even if no clocks were present. Ranking the finest competitions of the century is still a daunting task. but at least the standards for comparison are more fair: excitement and significance.

This is not a collection of great performances, per se, but a collection of great battles, both the exciting and the historically significant. Roger Bannister's historic sub-4:00 mile didn't make the grade; it was little more than a glorified time trial. His epic race against rival John Landy at the Empire Games later that summer, however, is a classic that is included.

You'll find precious few rabbited races on the list. You will also probably find a North American bias here, though the main focus is on international competition. What you won't find is equality. World-class track for women didn't come close to matching men's track until the 1960s, so the fairer sex has only had four decades of the century to work with. (Fanny Blankers-Koen, the star of the 1948 Games, is the notable exception. Babe Didrikson in 1932? Overrated.)

"Why, oh why?!" you might demand when faced with some of my omissions. The answer probably is that your favorite -- be it Bannister's first sub-four minute mile, Flojo's 10.49-second sprint, or Beamon's world-record long jump -- wasn't really a great competition. Great performance by an individual? Sure. But a great competition involves some level of uncertainty or surprise about who will win the event, at least for most of its duration.

### The specter of drugs
One of the realities of modern athletics is that drugs plays a role. To what extent, no one truly knows--at least, no one person has a grasp of the entire picture. And like other social ills--racism, for example--the specter of drugs affects everyone in the sport in some way, in much the same way that racism is among us, and even if we are not racist, we can surely acknowledge that has a real effect on our society.

I have included at least two competitions whose results were later changed because of drug disqualifications. This book is about the excitement of the competition. To write about that competition post-disqualification--and completely ignore the person who crossed the line first--is to participate in a delusional act of revisionist history. So I tried to call those events the way I saw them at the time.

In other cases, there are athletes mentioned in these pages who later ran afoul of the drug-testing authorities. Sometimes I mentioned this; sometimes not. To brand them all as heathens would also be disingenuous, as legion are those who have slipped through the drug dragnet uncaught. We sometimes refer to the latter individuals as "heroes."

### The future of competition
For the next 100 years, providing great competitions may prove to be one of the sport's greatest challenges. They can still be found in abundance at many levels in the sport, from age-group races to college championships. At the elite level, however, we are still seeing more big stars ducking each other, as well as the numbing over-reliance on rabbited distance races in most invitationals.

A sport that devotes itself single-mindedly to the pursuit of records will surely disenchant most fans because the majority of record chases inevitably end in failure. Meanwhile, the pursuit itself costs the sport its very soul; the hard-fought world-class competitions from which the sport once sprang are becoming novelties, granted to us lowly fans only when the powerful business managers decide that the price is right.

So here, for the sake of argument, are the 100 greatest competitions of this century. --*Jeff Hollobaugh*

# No. 100 -- Olympic Men's 5,000, Stockholm 1912: Kolehmainen vs Bouin

France's Jean Bouin won his heat in 15:05.0 (the world record at the time was 15:01.2). He pounded through the final at breakneck pace, burning off all of his competitors except Finland's Hannes Kolehmainen, who had won the 10,000 two days earlier. Journalists clocked the two in 8:46 at 3,000m, better than the world record. On the last lap, Kolehmainen pulled even and the two hammered away at each other. They passed three miles in 14:07.2, a full 10 seconds better than the world record.

With 20 meters left, Kolehmainen finally edged ahead. He crossed the line in 14:36.6, a world record by 24.6 seconds. Bouin, a tenth behind, captured the silver. Bronze medallist George Hutson of Britain ran one of the fastest times in history (15:07.6), but finished an astounding half-lap back. At the time, Kolehmainen's Finland was controlled by Russia, and for his gold medal ceremony, the Russian flag was raised. He later said he "almost wished" he hadn't won.

Kolehmainen returned to the Olympics after World War I to win the 1920 marathon gold. For years the bricklayer resided and competed in the United States as a member of the Irish American AC. He even enlisted in the New York National Guard and in 1921, was granted U.S. citizenship. He died in Finland in 1966.

Bouin wasn't as fortunate as his rival. He was killed in World War I in the fighting in 1914 near Xivray, Meuse, at age 25.

## FINAL RESULTS (7/10)
1. Hannes Kolehmainen (Finland) ........................ 14:36.6 world record
2. Jean Bouin (France) .......................................... 14:36.7
3. George Hutson (Great Britain) ......................... 15:07.6
4. George Bonhag (USA) ...................................... 15:09.8
5. Tel Berna (USA) ............................................... 15:10.0
6. Mauritz Carlsson (Sweden) ............................. 15:18.6
7. Henry Louis Scott (USA) .................................. nt
8. Alexander Decoteau (Canada) .......................... nt

# No. 99 -- Olympic Women's 80m Hurdles, London 1948: Blankers-Koen vs. Gardner

On paper, the "Flying Dutchwoman," Fanny Blankers-Koen, figured to be the strong favorite. She had run a world record for the 100 (11.5) that season and had also notched the best in the 80 hurdles (11.0). Many, however, considered the 30-year-old mother of two to be too old to win the gold. In fact, her prime motivation was a quote she read of the British team manager saying exactly that.

In the final she faced Maureen Gardner, a 19-year-old with great promise. Gardner got a great start, and Blankers-Koen a horrible one. It wasn't until after hurdle four that she drew even to Gardner. Then, outrunning her step pattern, she slammed hurdle five. She later recalled, "It was a grim struggle, in which my hurdling style went to pieces. I staggered like a drunkard."

Amazingly, Blankers-Koen hit the finish just inches ahead of Gardner, as both were timed in 11.2, an Olympic record.

Blankers-Koen stayed active in athletics for several more years, but her appearance in the 1952 Games only yielded a did-not-finish in the hurdles. In 1999, she was honored by the International Association of Athletics Federations as its "Female Athlete of the Century." She did in 2004 at age 85.

## FINAL RESULTS (8/4)
1. Fanny Blankers-Koen (Netherlands)................................. 11.2
2. Maureen Gardner (Great Britain) ..................................... 11.2
3. Shirley Strickland (Australia) ......................................... 11.4
4. Yvette Monginou (France) ............................................... 11.8
5. Maria Oberbreyer-Trösch (Austria) .................................. 11.8
6. Libuše Lomská (Czechoslovakia) ...................................... 11.9

# No. 98 -- Olympic Men's Shot, Seoul 1988: Timmerman vs. Gunthor

East German Ulf Timmermann, the world record holder at 75 feet, 8 inches (23.06), entered the competition as the strong favorite, as Swiss rival Werner Gunthor had been weakened by flu. In the first three rounds, Timmermann threw three Olympic records, topped by a 72-8½ (22.16). Gunthor could only manage a 71-2½ (21.70), and American phenomenon Randy Barnes, "in a daze," had a best of only 67-11¾ (20.72).

In round five, Gunthor scared Timmermann with a 72-1¾ (21.99). The East German responded with another Olympic record, 73-1¾ (22.29). Then Barnes "decided to get reckless" with his final throw. He spun at full speed, and hurled the shot out to 73-5½ (22.39) to take the lead. After two others finished off, Timmermann stepped into the ring for the final throw of the day. He popped a monster 73-8¾ (22.47), an Olympic record that still stands today. "Now I have gray hair," he said.

Barnes, still a youngster in 1988 at age 22, produced some fantastic results in his later career, but also was no stranger to scandal. In 1989, he threw 74-4¼ (22.66) for an indoor world record, and in 1990 he broke the outdoor record with a toss of 75-10¼ (23.12). However he tested positive for a steroid later that summer and because of that missed the 1992 Games. He finally won Olympic gold in 1996, coming from behind with a 70-11¼ final throw. Two years later he hit another drug ban that effectively ended his career.

## FINAL RESULTS (9/23)

1. Ulf Timmermann (East Germany).....................73-8¾     (22.47)
(22.02/72-3, 21.31/69-11, 22.16/72-8½, 21.90/71-10¼, 22.29/73-1¾, 22.47/73-8¾)
2. Randy Barnes (USA)...........................................73-5½     (22.39)
(20.17/66-2¼, 20.72/67-11¾, f, 21.31/69-11, 21.01/68-11¼, 22.39/73-5½)
3. Werner Günthör (Switzerland)..........................72-1¾     (21.99)
(21.45/70-4½, 21.59/70-10, 21.70/71-2½, 20.98/68-10, 21.99/72-1¾, 21.61/70-10¾)
4. Udo Beyer (East Germany)................................70-2½     (21.40)
5. Remigius Machura (Czechoslovakia).................67-6     (20.57)
6. Gert Weil (Chile)................................................66-10½     (20.38)
7. Alessandro Andrei (Italy)..................................66-9¾     (20.36)
8. Sergey Smirnov (Soviet Union)..........................66-9¾     (20.36)

# No. 97 -- Olympic Men's Steeplechase, Helsinki 1952: Ashenfelter vs. Kazantsev

Do the math ... the world record, set by the Soviet Union's Vladimir Kazantsev that year, was 8:48.6. FBI agent Horace Ashenfelter, who reportedly trained by leaping over park benches, had a best of only 9:06.4. Serious underdog territory. Still, Ashenfelter shocked by winning his heat with an American record 8:51.0. Then in the final, only the sixth steeple of his career, the Penn State alum outsprinted Kazantsev to steal the gold in a world record 8:45.4. (It was automatically timed at 8:45.68, but in accordance with the rules of the time, the hand time was the one that was recognized as the record.)

The event won Ashenfelter much fame because it occurred at the height of the Cold War, and an FBI agent's victory over a Soviet would not go unnoticed. Also notable was the fact that Ashenfelter had served as a fighter pilot for the U.S. Army Air Corps during World War II. Kazantsev had served in the Soviet Army on the Eastern Front.

Eventually Ashenfelter won a total of 17 national titles. He left the FBI and finished his business career as a precious metals salesman. Into his 80s, he was still playing golf regularly.

## FINAL RESULTS (7/25)
1. Horace Ashenfelter (USA) ........................8:45.4 (8:45.68)
2. Vladimir Kazantsev (Soviet Union) ..........8:51.6 (8:51.52)
3. John Disley (Great Britain) ......................8:51.8 (8:51.94)
4. Olavi Rinteenpää (Finland) ......................8:55.2 (8:55.58)
5. Curt Söderberg (Sweden)..........................8:55.6 (8:55.87)
6. Günthor Hesselmann (West Germany).....8:55.8 (8:55.97)
7. Mikhail Saltykov (Soviet Union)..............8:56.2 (8:56.47)
8. Helmut Gude (West Germany) ................9:01.4 (9:01.36)

# No. 96 -- Olympic Trials Men's 400m Hurdles, Stanford 1932: Hardin vs. Beatty

Glenn Hardin
[*Louisiana State University*]

Running in the fifth 400 hurdles race of his life, LSU's Glenn Hardin barely made it to the final, qualifying out of lane one in his semi thanks to a desperate final sprint. Favored Eugene Beatty, the fastest hurdler in the world up to that point, led most of the final, with Hardin well back. On the last hurdle, however, Beatty fell. Hardin charged, moving from third place into the lead to claim victory in 53.5. Or so he thought. AAU officials disqualified him for running out of his lane, so he was denied the national title. But he was still declared the winner of the Trials ... go figure.

At the Los Angeles Olympics the next month, Hardin won silver with his world record 51.9. That's right. The winner, Ireland's Bob Tisdall (51.7), ran even faster but was denied record credit because he had knocked over a hurdle.

In 1936, Hardin finally won a gold medal. He would retire with a four-year undefeated streak. His 1934 world record of 50.6 would last nearly 20 years. Years later, his son Billy Hardin would compete in the 1964 Tokyo Olympics in the same event. In 1975, the elder Hardin died of a heart attack.

## FINAL RESULTS (7/16)
1. Glenn Hardin (Louisiana St) ............................................. 53.5 (53.54)
2. Joseph Healey (New York AC) ............................................ 53.9
3. F. Morgan Taylor (Illinois AC) .......................................... 54.3
did not finish -- Eugene Beatty (Michigan Normal School)

# No. 95 -- Olympic Men's 400m, Rome 1960: Davis vs Kaufmann

Otis Davis attended Tuscaloosa Industrial High in Alabama in the 1950s, at a time when the high schools were still segregated by race. "They didn't have a track team," he says. "They only had basketball and football." So he played, and not particularly well. "I weighed 127 pounds when I graduated." Davis joined the Air Force, where he grew taller and stronger, and afterwards his love of basketball drew him to LA City College. "We had a good team," he remembers. "We won 34 games." Then he transferred to the University of Oregon on a basketball scholarship.

One day, while wandering around campus, Davis met Hall of Fame coach Bill Bowerman. "I saw them running at the track and I asked Bowerman if he needed any athletes. He said he needed high jumpers. Well, one thing led to another." Yet he told Bowerman, "You'll never make a runner out of me."

No high jumper, Davis started sprinting at age 25. It went well. "I had played basketball for a year at Oregon, and then I had to make a choice. I felt I couldn't do both. I chose track. I had begun to realize that while I could play basketball well, I wouldn't be a pro. And I knew I could run track after college."

In 1960, he won the national AAU title in the 400, his strong finish giving him a 45.8 clocking. Then came the Olympic Trials. "I was still learning to run the event," he says. He clocked 46.0 in the semis, and then charged from behind in the finals to snatch third in 46.7.

Over the next few months, the Olympic coaches had him race from a variety of lanes in the 400, so he could see the race from different angles. "I was literally learning on my way to the Games." A panel of six experts formcharted the race before the Games, and only two of them had Davis getting a medal, and they thought it would be bronze.

In Rome, Davis finished like a freight train to win the first round in 46.8. In the second round, he ran 45.9. Then came the semis, and the neophyte started raising some eyebrows by clocking an Olympic record 45.5. In the next day's final, Davis made his move early and held a big lead coming off the turn. "I started my kick a long ways from home, farther than I ever have," he told reporters.

Favored Carl Kaufmann chased hard, narrowing the gap with each stride. The German dove for the finish, while Davis swiveled his head to see how close he came. The judges needed the photofinish picture to decide. Davis had won by a hundredth of a second, as for the first time in history, the 45-second barrier had been broken. Both Davis and Kaufmann clocked 44.9. (The actual FAT times, widely disregarded at the time, gave Davis a 45.07 and Kaufmann 45.08.)

Two days later, Davis stood in the exchange zone for the anchor leg of the 4 x 400 relay. Next to him stood Kaufmann, anxious for revenge. The United States had led Germany from the start, and third leg Glenn Davis (no relation), had stretched the margin from a few feet to five yards. The Davis's shared a terrific pass, gaining another yard on their rivals. Yet Kaufmann was not finished. The Brooklyn-born German came up on Davis's heels on the last turn, then saw Davis put the jets on. A stunning acceleration produced a four-yard gap for Davis, and Kaufman could not respond. He anchored the Germans to a time a full second under the world record, but the Americans finished another half-second ahead in 3:02.2. Davis split 45.0 to Kaufman's 44.9.

Said Davis of his two golds and two world records, "I just learned how to run in the last couple of races." It was only the third track season of his life.

These days he lives in New Jersey and directs Safe Haven, an after-school sports program for kids ages 8-12. "It's tied in with drug prevention. I concentrate on the kids who are left out." He is also president of the Tri-States Olympians, and was selected to be in the United States Olympic Committees Project Gold 2000, an initiative to increase involvement of minorities and women in the Olympics.

# FINAL RESULTS (9/6)
1. Otis Davis (USA) ....................................... 44.9 (45.07)
2. Carl Kaufmann (West Germany) .............. 44.9 (45.08)
3. Malcolm Spence (South Africa) ................. 45.5 (45.60)
4. Milkha Singh (India) ................................. 45.6 (45.73)
5. Manfred Kinder (West Germany) .............. 45.9 (46.04)
6. Earl Young (USA) ..................................... 45.9 (46.07)

# No. 94 -- Weltklasse Women's 100, Zurich 1984: Ashford vs. Göhr

Evelyn Ashford versus Marlies Göhr, one of the great rivalries in the history of the sprints. East Germany's Göhr had won their last two matchups before the Olympics. But she was denied the chance to race Ashford in Los Angeles because of the Soviet-led boycott of the Games.

Ashford won the gold in 10.97, while Göhr won the Eastern Bloc "Friendship Games" in 10.95. They met to settle the score at the world's premier invitational, Zurich's Weltklasse. Göhr took command at the start, getting a full meter on her rival by the 20-meter mark. Ashford ran confidently, and at 60 meters pulled even. Göhr stiffened, while observers noted how relaxed Ashford ran. A final burst by the East German fell short. "I could sense that Göhr was even with me," said Ashford. "I knew I just had to relax and pull away." She did, clocking a world record 10.76 to Göhr's 10.84.

Ashford continued competing into the 1990s, winning her fourth Olympic gold medal (1 @ 100m, 3 @ 4 x 100m) at the 1992 Barcelona Games.

## FINAL RESULTS (8/22)
1. Evelyn Ashford (USA)................................10.76   world record
2. Marlies Göhr (East Germany) ..................10.84
3. Diane Williams (USA) ..............................11.04
4. Ingrid Auerswald (East Germany)............11.04
5. Silke Gladisch (East Germany).................11.11
6. Angela Bailey (Canada)............................11.25
7. Rose-Aimee Bacoul (France) .....................11.34
8. Grace Jackson (Jamaica) ..........................11.89

# No. 93 -- Olympic Men's 5,000, Barcelona 1992: Baumann vs. the Kenyans

By the 1990s, Africans ruled the distance running world. At the previous summer's World Champs, they won 11 of 12 medals from 1,500 to 10,000 meters. German Dieter Baumann, a silver medalist in the 1988 Games, had honed his finishing kick to challenge them. He looked good in the heats, leading with a 13:20.82.

Observers figured the Kenyans would use team tactics, with one of them forcing the pace to take the sting away from the kickers. Dominic Kirui drew that straw but wasn't up to the task, fading after two kilometers. Teammate Yobes Ondieki took over for the next two kilometers,

On the last lap, Baumann found himself badly boxed in. When his four African rivals started their sprints, he had nowhere to go. On the last turn, he realized he had to gamble. He hit the brakes to escape the box from the rear, and then ran wide to start passing the others. He moved into the lead with only 12 meters left, and won the gold by a stride in 13:12.52. His last 200? A dazzling 24.9 that included his escape act.

Baumann continued to produce great races throughout the rest of his career, placing 4th in the 1996 Olympics and later becoming the first European to break 13 minutes for the 5000m in 1997. In 1999, his biography lurched into the bizarre toothpaste scandal, when he busted for using the steroid nandrolone. The German federation accepted his explanation that an unknown malefactor had drugged his toothpaste, but the IAAF still kept him from competing in the 2000 Games. He finally retired from running in 2003.

Runner-up Bitok again won silver in the 1996 Olympics, while his wife, Pauline Konga, captured the gold in the women's race.

## FINAL RESULTS (8/8)
1. Dieter Baumann (Germany) ............................ 13:12.52
2. Paul Bitok (Kenya) .......................................... 13:12.71
3. Fita Bayissa (Ethiopia) .................................... 13:13.03
4. Brahim Boutayeb (Morocco) ............................. 13:13.27
5. Yobes Ondieki (Kenya) .................................... 13:17.50
6. Worku Bikila (Ethiopia) ................................... 13:23.52
7. Rob Denmark (Great Britain) .......................... 13:27.76
8. Abel Antón (Spain) .......................................... 13:27.80

# No. 92 — Commonwealth Games Men's 1500, Christchurch 1974: Bayi vs. Walker

Tanzanian Filbert Bayi surprised no one when he blistered the early pace, with only Mike Boit trying to keep up. Through 400 in 54.9, and 800 in 1:52.2, Bayi charged. Much farther back ran Kenyan Ben Jipcho, who had won the Commonwealth gold twice. Olympic bronze medalist Rod Dixon also gave chase, and farther back ran his New Zealand teammate, John Walker.

At three laps (2:50.8), Boit had faded, and Jipcho mounted a doomed effort. Walker and Dixon soon passed him, and on the final turn, everyone waited for Bayi to crumble from the suicidal pace. It never happened. As Walker drew close on the homestretch, Bayi glanced at him and sprinted away. He crossed the line victorious in 3:32.2 as both he and Walker (3:32.5) broke Jim Ryun's world record of 3:33.1. So thrilled was Bayi that he launched into an all-out sprint on his victory lap.

In 1975, Walker would become the first man in history to break 3:50 in the mile. He would go on to win the 1976 Olympic gold medal, one of many hoped-for clashes between the two that never materialized. He finally retired from running after 1990, and now runs an equestrian shop in Auckland.

Bayi was denied the chance to run in Montreal because of the African boycott of the Games. After his retirement from sports, he put together the Filbert Bayi Foundation to guide young talent in Tanzania. The foundation also works to educate the young about HIV and AIDS. He has also founded several schools in Tanzania.

## FINAL RESULTS (2/2)

1. Filbert Bayi (Tanzania)        3:32.2  (3:32.16)  world record
2. John Walker (New Zealand)      3:32.5  (3:32.52)
3. Ben Jipcho (Kenya)             3:33.1  (3:33.16)
4. Rod Dixon (New Zealand)        3:33.9  (3:33.89)
5. Graham Crouch (Australia)      3:34.2  (3:34.22)
6. Mike Boit (Kenya)              3:36.8  (3:36.84)
7. Brendan Foster (Great Britain) 3:37.6  (3:37.64)
8. Suleiman Nyambui (Tanzania)    3:39.6

# No. 91 -- World Championships Women's 400 Hurdles, Stuttgart 1993: Gunnell vs. Farmer-Patrick

American Sandra Farmer-Patrick wanted to improve upon her silver medal at the previous year's Olympics. She worked herself into the best shape of her life, and ran this race as if her life depended upon it.

She charged into the lead at the first hurdle, and by hurdle four had a clear lead over her rival, Olympic champion Sally Gunnell. That margin slowly shrank, and as Gunnell blasted the second turn, she edged into the lead. Farmer-Patrick responded by sprinting back into the lead after hurdle No. 8. Gunnell, however, never let up, coming from a clear deficit at the last hurdle. She chewed away at the lead and passed the American several strides from the finish.

Gunnell (52.74) and Farmer-Patrick (52.79) both went under the world record of 52.94. Said the Briton, "I couldn't be sure that I had won, so I didn't start celebrating in case I made a fool of myself."

After her retirement in 1997, Gunnell went on to become a well-known commentator and TV personality in Britain.

## FINAL RESULTS (8/19)
1. Sally Gunnell (Great Britain) ............. 52.74   world record
2. Sandra Farmer-Patrick (USA)............ 52.79   American record
3. Margarita Ponomaryova (Russia) ....... 53.48
4. Kim Batten (USA)............................... 53.84
5. Tonja Buford (USA) ........................... 54.55
6. Deon Hemmings (Jamaica)................. 54.99
7. Rosey Edeh (Canada)......................... 55.19
8. Natalya Torshina (Kazakhstan).......... 55.78

# No. 90 -- Bislett Men's 1,500, Oslo 1981: Byers shocks Ovett

It was the summer of the mile, and the British ruled. Sebastian Coe and Steve Ovett lorded over the world's 1,500-meter men and spent much of the summer ducking each other. With Coe absent, Ovett, who had set a mile world record at Bislett the previous year, figured to win easily.

On the first lap, American Tom Byers, who had been asked to supply a fast pace, broke away from the pack with a steady surge. Ovett and company decided the one-time wunderkind was going too fast, so they weren't going to go with him. At 400 meters, the pack heard a 57.6-second split, with Byers more than 10 meters ahead. Then at 800, they heard a split of 1:54.9, and Byers was an astounding 40 meters-plus ahead. He was out of his mind, they figured.

When the pack hit 1,200 and heard 2:53.0, they collectively realized that they must have been hearing Byers' splits all along, since no one could be 60 meters ahead of a 2:53.0. The chase began. Ovett ripped through his last lap (52.3) in full panic mode. He had cut Byers' lead in half by the time he hit the home stretch; he would run the final 200 in 24.5. Byers grimly held on, his leaden legs clocking 61.5 for his last circuit. He hit the line in 3:39.01, just ahead of Ovett's 3:39.53, becoming the third man in four years to defeat the Brit in his main event. "I don't think they'd let it happen again," said Byers.

Quipped Ovett, "We ran like a load of hacks."

## FINAL RESULTS (6/26)
1. Tom Byers (USA)................................................3:39.01
2. Steve Ovett (Great Britain) ..............................3:39.53
3. José Luiz González (Spain)...............................3:39.58
4. Steve Scott (USA) ..............................................3:39.59
5. Steve Cram (Great Britain) ..............................3:40.48
6. Todd Harbour (USA)...........................................3:40.85
7. Richie Harris (USA)............................................3:41.16
8. Thomas Wessinghage (West Germany) ..............3:41.35

# No. 89 -- Olympic Men's Shot, Amsterdam 1928: Kuck Surprises All

Though Kansan Johnny Kuck had thrown a world record 51 feet- ½ inch(15.55) early in the year, the big favorite for Olympic gold was Emil Hirschfeld of Germany, who had popped a 51-9¾ (15.79)a week later.

In Amsterdam, Hirschfeld, obviously in top form, launched the iron ball out to 51-7 (15.72), but couldn't match the 51-8¼ (15.75) thrown earlier by Kuck's teammate, Herman Brix.

Kuck, who was known to throw some monster throws in practice, always had great difficulty putting it together for a big meet. Overcome by nerves, he went to teammate Brix and asked for help. As Brix remembered years later, "He came to me and said, 'I don't know what the dickens to do. This is terrible.' I said, 'Well, I suggest that you lie down here on the field (it was a nice warm day) in your sweat clothes, and imagine you're back home on the farm in Kansas. And when you hear your name called, imagine it's your dad and mother sitting on the porch and they want to see you put the shot. Forget the crowd, forget where you are, forget everything and just get up and show your mom and dad how you do it.' "

Then Kuck, who had only been third in the Olympic Trials, surprised everyone with his world record 52-¾ (15.87) to steal the gold.

After the Games, Hirschfeld boosted his self-esteem with a binge of three world records, topped by a 52-7½ (16.04), but Kuck would always have the gold. Brix, meanwhile, changed his name to Bruce Bennett and went on to play Tarzan in several movies.

## FINAL RESULTS (7/29)

| | | |
|---|---|---|
| 1. Johnny Kuck (USA) | 15.87 | 52-¾ |
| 2. Herman Brix (USA) | 15.75 | 51-8¼ |
| 3. Emil Hirschfeld (Germany) | 15.72 | 51-7 |
| 4. Eric Krenz (USA) | 14.99 | 49-2¼ |
| 5. Armas Wahlstedt (Finland) | 14.69 | 48-2½ |
| 6. Wilhelm Uebler (Germany) | 14.69 | 48-2½ |
| 7. Harlow Rothert (USA) | 14.68 | 48-2 |
| 8. József Darányi (Hungary) | 14.35 | 47-1 |

# No. 88 -- World Championships Men's 4-x-400 Relay, Athens 1997: Pettigrew Ignites Last Leg

The 4-x-4 may be a traditionally strong American event, but in Athens all bets were off. Michael Johnson and Butch Reynolds couldn't run because of injury. That left Antonio Pettigrew as the sole veteran on the squad, and he was still taking the rap for the loss to the British in 1991.

Meanwhile, the British lined up their silver medal squad from Atlanta, and the Jamaicans put forth a dangerous team as well. U.S. lead-off Jerome Young clocked a 44.6 and handed off just behind the Jamaicans. Then Pettigrew set about redeeming his reputation. He ran the best lap of his great career, giving the U.S. an eight-meter lead with his 43.1, the second-fastest relay leg in history.

Third leg Chris Jones was passed by the British during his 44.8 circuit, but came back to hand off to anchor Tyree Washington with a four-meter lead. Washington maintained that lead until the home stretch, when Britain's Mark Richardson came even. Then Washington fought back, handing the United States the gold in 2:56.47, with the Brits a stride behind in 2:56.65. The Jamaicans, just a tenth back, produced a national record 2:56.75.

In 2008, as part of the trial of coach Trevor Graham, Pettigrew admitted taking performance-enhancing drugs. The 2000 Olympic 4 x 400 team that he was on was stripped of its medals. Though his earlier results were not affected by that decision, Pettigrew voluntarily returned other medals he had won in the period in question.

In August 2010, Pettigrew--then an assistant coach at North Carolina--was found dead in his car. The autopsy ruled he had committed suicide by overdose.

## FINAL RESULTS (8/10)

DQ - United States ........................................ 2:56.47
(Jerome Young 45.2, Antonio Pettigrew 43.7, Chris Jones 44.71, Allen Johnson 46.19)
1. Great Britain ............................................. 2:56.65
2. Jamaica .................................................... 2:56.75
3. Poland ...................................................... 3:00.26
4. South Africa............................................... 3:00.26
5. France....................................................... 3:01.06
6. Zimbabwe ................................................. 3:01.43
7. Italy......................................................... 3:01.52

# No. 87 -- Olympic Men's High Jump, Atlanta 1996: Austin over Partyka

When Charles Austin missed his second attempt at 7-9¼ (2.37), he faced a dilemma. Poland's Artur Partyka had made that height on his second try. That meant that the Pole had the lead, and all Austin could be assured of was silver.

Austin could have chosen to jump at 7-9¼ (2.37) a third time. That would be his best chance to earn three more jumps at the next height. Or, he could pass to an Olympic record 7-10 (2.39), where he would have only one chance to win the gold.

Austin passed, as did Britain's Steve Smith, in third place. At 7-10 (2.39), Partyka missed. Then, with the running events concluded and a crowded stadium chanting only for him, Austin produced the perfect jump, sailing over to claim the first U.S. win in the event since 1968. After Partyka and Smith exhausted their remaining efforts, Austin celebrated with three unsuccessful tries for a world record 8-¾ (2.46).

After his retirement from competition, Austin opened up the So High Sports and Fitness Performance Center in San Marcos, Texas, and has produced several books and videos.

## FINAL RESULTS (7/28)
1. Charles Austin (USA) ................................ 7-10     (2.39)
2. Artur Partyka (Poland) ............................ 7-9¼     (2.37)
3. Steve Smith (Great Britain) ...................... 7-8½     (2.35)
4. Dragutin Topić (Yugoslavia) ..................... 7-7¼     (2.32)
5. Steinar Hoen (Norway) ........................... 7-7¼     (2.32)
6. Lambros Papakostas (Greece) ................... 7-7¼     (2.32)
7. Tim Forsyth (Australia) ........................... 7-7¼     (2.32)
8. Lee Jin-Taek (South Korea) ...................... 7-6     (2.29)

# No. 86 — World Championships Women's Javelin, Helsinki 1983: Lillak vs. Whitbread

The very first of the IAAF's World Championships meant a lot to the Finns, since they were the host nation. Not surprisingly, the best of Finnish athletes faced tremendous pressure to win the gold.

Such was Tiina Lillak's lot. The world record-holder at 245-3 (74.76), Lillak had been labelled a "choker" after failing to win a medal at the previous summer's European champs. Here, she put herself into medal position with a first round 220-11 (67.34), but the wind didn't favor long throws, and Britain's Fatima Whitbread had a big lead with her 226-10 (69.14).

Then hurdler Arto Bryggare won a silver medal for Finland. On his celebration lap, he and Lillak shared an emotional hug, then she approached the runway inspired to launch the spear to victory. It landed at 221-4 (67.46), an improvement, but not even close to gold. That left her only one throw. When Whitbread passed her last attempt, Lillak responded to the crowd's cheers and threw the javelin far, very far. It hit 232-4 (70.82), and Finland finally had its gold medal.

## FINAL RESULTS (8/13)

1. Tiina Lillak (Finland) .................................. 70.82         232-4
2. Fatima Whitbread (Great Britain).............. 69.14         226-10
3. Anna Verouli (Greece) ............................... 65.72         215-7
4. Tessa Sanderson (Great Britain) ................ 64.76         212-5
5. Éva Rádouly-Zörgö (Romania) .................... 63.86         209-6
6. Tuula Laaksalo (Finland) ........................... 62.44         204-10
7. Beate Peters (West Germany).................... 62.42         204-9
8. María Colón (Cuba) ................................... 62.04         203-6

# No. 85 -- Olympic Men's 10,000, Munich 1972: Viren Bounces Back

The longest track race generated great excitement in the qualifying heats (the first since 1920). All 15 qualifiers to the final bettered Billy Mills' Olympic record of 28:24.4, led by Belgian Emiel Puttemans (27:53.4) and Britain's Dave Bedford (27:53.6).

All eyes focused on Bedford, a great talent who had earned the label "unpredictable." Sure enough, he took the race out at an unheard-of pace, hitting 4:15 at the mile. The long pack, all running at a world-record clip, stayed with him. Then, approaching the halfway mark, Finland's Lasse Viren inadvertently caused a collision. He went down, with Tunisian veteran Mohamed Gammoudi tumbling over him onto the infield.

Viren sat dazed for a few seconds, then jumped to his feet and started chasing the pack. Gammoudi came up more slowly, and ran a lap and a half before dropping out. In the final kilometer, only five remained in the running. A lap later, Viren moved to the front with a dazzling burst, dropping American hope Frank Shorter as Puttemans and Ethiopia's Miruts Yifter gave chase.

No one, however, expected Viren to summon a 1:56.4 for the last two laps, a finishing drive unheard of in 10,000-meter running back then. He crossed the line in 27:38.4, breaking Ron Clarke's 1965 world record of 27:39.4 by a second and giving Finland its first gold since 1936.

## FINAL RESULTS (9/3)

1. Lasse Viren (Finland) .................... 27:38.4 (27:38.35) world record
2. Emiel Puttemans (Belgium)........... 27:39.6 (27:39.58)
3. Miruts Yifter (Ethiopia) ................. 27:41.0 (27:40.96)
4. Mariano Haro (Spain) .................... 27:48.2 (27:48.14)
5. Frank Shorter (USA) ..................... 27:51.4 (27:51.32)
6. David Bedford (Great Britain) ....... 28:05.4 (28:05.44)
7. Daniel Korica (Yugoslavia) ............ 28:15.2 (28:15.18)
8. Abdelkader Zaddem (Tunisia)........ 28:18.2 (28:18.17)

# No. 84 -- AAU Men's 1,500, Milwaukee 1934: Bonthron vs. Cunningham

Bill Bonthron [National Library of New Zealand']

Princeton's Bill Bonthron and mile legend Glenn Cunningham shared a fierce rivalry in 1934. That spring, 25,000 fans watched as Cunningham demolished Bonthron on his home track at the Princeton Invitational, winning in a world record 4:06.7. Bonthron came back at the NCAA Champs and beat Cunningham with a 4:08.9.

Then came the U.S. national championships. After a fast 61.3 opener in the 100-degree heat, Cunningham moved hard on the second lap, hitting the halfway point in an unprecedented 2:01.8.

Bonthron couldn't hang with that pace, and was 11 yards back as the two neared the three-quarter mark. Cunningham clocked 3:04.5 there and continued to pull away. By the final turn, he had 15 yards on his rival.

Then Bonthron entered the homestretch and exploded into a furious sprint, which some called his "bicycle" finish. He ran down Cunningham in stunning fashion, passing him 20 yards from the tape. A stride before the finish, Bothron glanced back as if to confirm his victory. He won in 3:48.8, .1 ahead of Cunningham, as both broke the world record.

Said Cunningham, "It's a strange feeling to break a world record and lose." Bonthron, exhausted by his effort, collapsed and never made it to the victory stand.

## FINAL RESULTS (6/30)
1. Bill Bonthron (Princeton) ................ 3:48.8   world record
2. Glenn Cunningham ......................... 3:48.9
3. Gene Venzke.................................... 3:50.5
4. Robert Morris ................................. nt

# No. 83 -- Olympic Women's 100, Berlin 1936: Stephens vs. Walsh

Helen Stephens came to the Berlin Olympics as a sprinter who had never been beaten in the 100. The six-foot tall Missouri farm girl had started her career when her high school gym teacher had clocked her in a world record for the 50-yard dash during a fitness test. In her first official race, she tied the world indoor record for 50 yards and beat Stella Walsh, the Olympic champion.

In Berlin she faced Polish star Walsh (originally Stanislawa Walesiewicz), whom she had earlier beaten to win the U.S. title. Though Stephens had clocked a 10.8 for 100 yards (the world record was 11.0), the German crowd was stunned when she crushed Walsh in a wind-aided 11.5 for 100 meters.

Helen Stephens [William Woods University]

Stephens later turned pro, racing against Jesse Owens and also playing with two women's pro basketball teams. Walsh, tragically, was murdered in 1980 and an autopsy revealed that she was a hermaphrodite, leading to controversy about the legitimacy of her many medals and records.

## FINAL RESULTS (8/4)
1. Helen Stephens (USA) ............................... 11.5
2. Stanislawa Walasiewicz (Poland) .............. 11.7
3. Käthe Krauss (Germany) ........................... 11.9
4. Marie Dollinger (Germany) ........................ 12.0
5. Annette Rogers (USA) ............................... 12.2
6. Emmy Albus (Germany) ............................ 12.3

# No. 82 -- Olympic Women's 100, Atlanta 1996: Devers vs Ottey

In an event that has seen more than its share of controversies over close finishes, this was a doozy. Not surprisingly, the usual suspects were involved.

American Gail Devers started in lane two, with Jamaican rival Merlene Ottey in lane three. The compact Devers nailed the best start, however, and her teammate, Gwen Torrence, also had an early lead on Ottey. However, by mid-race, Ottey's long legs pulled even. The three stars raced to the finish, with Torrence slipping into third -- just barely -- while to many eyes, Devers and Ottey hit the line dead-even.

A careful study of the finish photo revealed that Devers' left shoulder hit the line about a centimeter before Ottey's chest, giving her a margin of .004 of a second. The times: Devers 10.94, Ottey 10.94, Torrence 10.96. Ottey, who had lost a similar close finish to Devers at the 1993 Worlds, refused to accept the verdict. She would end her fabulous career without ever having won an individual Olympic gold.

In later years, Devers continued competing, running world-leading times for the indoor hurdles in 2007 at age 40. Ottey also set longevity records, competing for Slovenia from 2002 on and representing that nation on its relay team in the European Championships in 2010 at the age of 50.

## FINAL RESULTS (7/27)
1. Gail Devers (USA) .............................10.94
2. Merlene Ottey (Jamaica) .....................10.94
3. Gwen Torrence (USA)..........................10.96
4. Chandra Sturrup (Bahamas)...............11.00
5. Marina Trandenkova (Russia)............11.06
6. Natalya Voronova (Russia).................11.10
7. Mary Onyali (Nigeria) ........................11.13
8. Zhanna Pintusevich (Ukraine)............11.14

# No. 81 -- Olympic Men's 100, London 1948: Dillard Stuns

The story of this race begins with the high hurdles event at the U.S. championships. Harrison "Bones" Dillard had won 82 straight races in the highs when Bill Porter upset him to win the national title. At the Olympic Trials, Dillard was determined to avenge that loss, but when he hit the second hurdle, he started to press too hard. He hit three more barriers hard before stopping to watch Porter win the race en route to an Olympic gold medal.

The day before, however, Dillard had run in the 100-meter final, finishing third to make the Olympic team. He didn't have much of a shot to win a medal in the sprint, but it was the only shot he had.

Once in London, Dillard performed well, even if he was in the wrong race. In the first two rounds, he had produced the fastest times (10.4s). Still, in the final, all eyes focused on his teammates, Barney Ewell and Mel Patton, along with Panama's Lloyd LaBeach. Patton got a poor start on the wet cinder track, with Dillard getting the best. He led the whole way, and streaked across the line in an Olympic-record 10.3.

On the other side of the track, Ewell finished second in 10.4 and, mistakenly thinking he had won, broke into a celebratory dance. Autotimes for the race showed the first four finished in a space of 0.11 seconds. Four years later, in Helsinki, Dillard finally won his gold medal in the hurdles.

## FINAL RESULTS (7/31)
1. Harrison Dillard (USA)..................................10.3
2. Barney Ewell (USA)......................................10.4
3. Lloyd LaBeach (Panama).............................10.6
4. Alastair McCorquodale (Great Britain) .........nt
5. Mel Patton (USA)...........................................nt
6. McDonald Bailey (Great Britain)..................nt

# No. 80 -- Olympic Men's 1,500, Stockholm 1912:

## Jackson Stuns

The chronicler of the 1,500/mile, Cordner Nelson, wrote that the Stockholm 1,500 was "the greatest race ever run" until that time. American hopes ran high, as the U.S. dominated miling at that point, and seven of the runners in the final were from the U.S. Abel Kiviat, a teenager until just before the Games, had broken the world record three times that season, topped by a 3:55.8. Also in the field was defending champion Mel Sheppard and the world record-holder in the mile, John Paul Jones.

The race started at a modest 65-second pace, led by France's Henri Arnaud. Norman Taber, another American with strong medal hopes, then took the lead and sped up the pace. At the bell, Kiviat jumped him, followed by Taber and Jones. On the last turn, Sheppard and Britain's Arnold Jackson also joined the crowd on his heels, with Sweden's Edwin Wide closing fast.

Kiviat fought for the lead with Taber as the competitors neared the finish. Jackson, Jones and Wide cut down the margin. With 50 yards left, Jackson came even with them, as Jones and Wide started to fade. The British star summoned one last burst and captured the gold in 3:56.8. Kiviat and Taber both clocked 3:56.9, and the photo had to be reviewed before officials handed the silver to Kiviat.

Jackson, who went by Strode-Jackson in later years, was one of England's most decorated soldiers in World War I, and has the distinction of being the British Army's youngest-ever brigadier general (age 27). His three war wounds ended his hopes of continuing as a runner. He served as a member of the British delegation to the Paris Peace Conference in 1919. He later moved to the U.S., founded the Kentucky Derby Festival in 1935, and served on the staff of the governor of Kentucky during World War II. After his wife's death, he returned home to England where he died in 1972.

## FINAL RESULTS (7/10)
1. Arnold Jackson (Great Britain) ........................................ 3:56.8
2. Abel Kiviat (USA) ............................................................ 3:56.9
3. Norman Taber (USA) ...................................................... 3:56.9
4. John Paul Jones (USA) .................................................... 3:57.2
5. Ernst Wide (Sweden) ....................................................... 3:57.6
6. Philip Baker (Great Britain) ............................................ 4:01.0
7. John Zander (Sweden) ..................................................... 4:02.0
8. Walter McClure (USA) ..................................................... nt

# No. 79 -- Olympic Men's 4-x-400 Relay, Helsinki 1952: Jamaica vs. the United States

Four years earlier, Jamaican star Arthur Wint cried after a cramp forced him to stop running, ending his nation's hopes of beating the United States in the 4 x 400. In Helsinki, however, the same Jamaican foursome looked stronger than ever. They had placed 1-2-5 in the open 400, led by George Rhoden and former Illinois star Herb McKenley.

Wint ran 46.8 on lead-off, finishing a few steps behind American Ollie Matson's 46.7. Second leg Les Laing produced a 47.0 (his open best was 47.5), but still lost ground, as the U.S.'s Eugene Cole built up a huge lead with his 45.5 leg. That split was faster than the 400-meter world record at the time, 45.8.

McKenley ran the third leg for Jamaica. Two months earlier he was bed-bound with the mumps, losing 20 pounds. He had to battle anemia in his recovery. He had tried to withdraw from the Jamaican team, but officials told him to get to Helsinki anyway. His silver in the 400 proved he had miraculously regained his fitness.

Charles Moore tried to maintain the huge U.S. lead, splitting a fine 46.3. McKenley steadily cut down the lead with his long stride, and amazed the crowd by moving into the lead with his final steps. He split a jaw-dropping 44.6, the fastest lap in history.

On the last lap, Rhoden led 800 winner Mal Whitfield as both clocked 45.5, managing to hold him off for a Jamaican win in a world record 3:03.9. The U.S. clocked 3:04.0, as Germany (3:06.6) also broke the old best of 3:08.2.

## FINAL RESULTS (7/27)
1. Jamaica .............................................. 3:03.9 (3:04.04)
(Arthur Wint 46.8, Leslie Laing 47.0, Herb McKenley 44.6, George Rhoden 45.5)
2. United States..................................... 3:04.0 (3:04.19)
(Ollie Matson 46.7, Eugene Cole 45.5, Charles Moore 46.3, Mal Whitfield 45.5)
3. Germany............................................. 3:06.6 (3:06.77)
4. Canada .............................................. 3:09.3 (3:09.37)
5. Great Britain ..................................... 3:10.0 (3:10.22)
6. France................................................ 3:10.1 (3:10.32)

# No. 78 — World Championships Women's Pole Vault, Seville 1999: Dragila Perfect

Recent, yes, but nonetheless amazing was Stacy Dragila's world-record tying win in the recent World Championships. One reason it was so amazing was that the former Idaho State star seemed to be having such a bad day.

Ukrainian Anzhela Balakhnova cleared on her first attempts all night, while Dragila seemed to need two or three tries at each height. Finally, with the bar at a world record 15-1 (4.60), the Ukrainian joined Dragila in missing. On the second attempt, however, Dragila stunned with a perfect clearance. Balakhnova would need to match that to stay ahead, but the wind was gone from her sails.

History had repeated itself, for better and worse. In 1997 Dragila had won the first women's vault at the World Indoor Champs by tying the world record, only to be denied the record bonus money because she hadn't actually "broken" the record. She did the same in Seville, and was again denied the record bonus, with her prize money halved to $30,000 because the vault is "new."

After the 2009 World Championships, Dragila retired from big-time competition. She had also won gold in the 2000 Olympic Games and the 2001 World Championships.

## FINAL RESULTS (8/21)

1. Stacy Dragila (USA) ............................ 4.60    15-1   world record
2. Anzhela Balakhonova (Ukraine)........... 4.55    14-11
3. Tatiana Grigorieva (Australia) ............. 4.45    14-7¼
4. Zsuzsanna Szabó (Hungary) ................. 4.40    14-5¼
5. Nicole Humbert (Germany) .................. 4.40    14-5¼
=6. Pavla Hamácková (Czech Republic).... 4.40    14-5¼
=6. Daniela Bártová (Czech Republic) ...... 4.40    14-5¼
8. Yelena Belyakova (Russia) ................... 4.35    14-3¼

# No. 77 -- Wanamaker Mile, Millrose Games, New York 1950: Wilt vs. Gehrmann

"The longest mile in history," the late track historian Wally Donovan said of the fabled Wanamaker race of 1950. FBI agent Fred Wilt, typically a two-miler indoors, took the early lead and held on until the final lap. That's when rival Don Gehrmann of Wisconsin came back from a five-yard deficit and made it to the finish in a dead heat with Wilt.

The finish judges could not agree on the winner. Recalled Howard Schmertz to the New York Times, "Since it was a virtual dead heat, it was impossible to call the winner with the naked eye. Each of the officials had the same time for both runners: 4:09.3. We went to the Bulova photofinish camera for the final word, and it showed the head of one of the judges. In the tumult, the judge had accidentally moved in front of the finish line and obscured the line of the camera."

Finally, Asa Bushnell, the head judge, voted for Wisconsin's Gehrmann, who had gone undefeated in 1949. Wilt filed a protest with the local AAU committee, which reversed the decision.

Bushnell appealed to the Metropolitan AAU, but that organization turned him down, and left Wilt the "winner." Bushnell pursued his appeal to the national level, and a special committee declared Gehrmann the winner, a finding that was finalized by a vote of the entire AAU board of governers in a 304-108 vote at their national convention. Gehrmann was told he could keep the silver cup, 11 months after the race had started.

In 1952, incidentally, the two finished in another close one at the NYAC Games. Gehrmann was originally declared the winner, but a one-hour review of the photo led to the decision going in Wilt's favor this time.

## FINAL RESULTS (1/28)
1. Don Gehrmann (USA)..................... 4:09.3
2. Fred Wilt (USA).............................. 4:09.3
3. John Joe Barry (Ireland)................. 4:10.2

# No. 76 — AAU Champs 6 Mile, San Diego 1965: Mills vs. Lindgren

Never did a race match two runners so hugely popular. Billy Mills had shocked the world the previous summer by winning the Olympic gold in the 10,000 meters. Diminutive Gerry Lindgren, just 19, had defeated the Russians in 1964, and decided to risk his collegiate eligibility by defying the NCAA ban on collegiate competitors at the U.S. national championships.

Mills wanted to break the world record, Ron Clarke's 27:17.8, and pushed ahead with a blistering pace. He passed three miles in 13:39.8, with Lindgren dogging him every step. Occasionally the Washington State star would shoot into the lead, but he couldn't hold it: "The tempo was so fast."

Mills, his feet on fire, forged on, convinced that Lindgren's loud breathing meant he was about to drop out. Driving the crowd into a frenzy, the two built up to a fast finish, and Lindgren finally went for the win around the last turn. He could not pass Mills, however. He got within a foot of him and simply could do no more. The two fought that way to the finish.

Remember Lindgren in a 2011 interview with *YouthRunner.com*, "Around the final turn I dug deeper, tightened my turnover just a bit and started to pull away from Billy slowly. Then I started thinking! Billy was older; this was his last year as a runner. I was young and had lots of years ahead of me. I let up just a bit. In that moment Billy came back and even inched ahead just a little bit. No, I thought! If Billy is going to win this race it will be over my dead body! I powered back in the final 20 yards. At the finish line I thought I was ahead of Billy but the photo timer and the finish judges didn't know that."

Mills won, but both were credited with a world record 27:11.6.

## FINAL RESULTS (6/27)

| | | |
|---|---|---|
| 1. Billy Mills | 27:11.6 | world record |
| 2. Gerry Lindgren | 27:11.6 | world record |
| 3. Bill Morgan | 28:33.8 | |
| 4. Doug Rustad | 28:44.0 | |
| 5. Jerry Smartt | 29:33.4 | |
| 6. Gar Williams | 29:33.4 | |
| 7. Ed Winrow | 29:47.4 | |

# No. 75 — Olympic Trials Men's Long Jump, Indianapolis 1988: Lewis vs. Myricks

Was Carl Lewis ever better than he was at the 1988 Olympic Trials? In the long jump, he and rival Larry Myricks, the last person to beat him seven years earlier, produced one of history's epic matches.

Myricks led off with a 27-foot, eight-inch (8.43) jump, and Lewis managed 27-4½ (8.34). In the second round, Myricks improved to 28-¾ (8.55). Rain started falling, and before long the field was drenched with heavy rain as thunder boomed. With the crowd fleeing, Lewis stepped onto the runway, a picture of perfect concentration. Fearing that the rain wouldn't stop, he wanted to get one more good jump in. That he did, with a 28-2¼ (8.60) that took the lead.

"I jumped in the rain because my thought was that it wasn't going to stop raining so I'd better jump as well as I could before it got worse," Lewis told reporters.

When the rain died down, Myricks stepped up for his third jump, and produced a lifetime best of 28-8¼ (8.74). Had Lewis finally met his match? No. On his next jump, King Carl flew three-quarters of an inch farther. The final rounds saw Myricks leap a 28-¾ (8.55) and fade away, while Lewis produced a world record-scaring foul, and a 28-5¾ (8.68).

## FINAL RESULTS
1. Carl Lewis (Santa Monica TC).............. 8.76    28-9
2. Larry Myricks (Goldwin TC)................. 8.74    28-8¼
3. Mike Powell (unattached) ..................... 8.36w    27-5¼w
4. Gordon Laine (Lay Witnesses).............. 8.31w    27-3¼w
5. Mike Conley (Tyson TC) ....................... 8.23    27-0
6. Andre Ester (Mazda TC)....................... 8.09w    26-6½w
7. Ty Jefferson (Tyson TC)........................ 8.04    26-4½
8. Eric Metcalf (Texas)............................. 8.04    26-4½

# No. 74 -- World Championships Men's 100, Tokyo 1991: Lewis vs. Burrell

To some fans, this was the greatest 100 ever because of the times. Throw out the times, and this was still one of the best. Earlier in the season, Carl Lewis had seen his training partner, Leroy Burrell, break his world record at nationals with a 9.90.

That the super-hard Tokyo track would produce incredible times was confirmed in the early rounds. Lewis ran a wind-aided 9.80, along with a 9.93. Burrell ran 9.94, and Frank Fredericks a windy 9.89.

In the final, the third American, Dennis Mitchell caught a flyer. His reaction time of 0.90 should have signaled the starter that a false start had occurred, but the starter was not wearing the headset, and missed the telltale beep. The rules of the time gave the starter final authority anyway, and he evidently judged Mitchell's lightning start acceptable.

Jamaican Raymond Stewart soon reeled in Mitchell, and Leroy Burrell came up behind him at halfway, with Lewis still well back. Burrell moved into the lead at 60 meters, while Lewis began moving past the rest of the field. In the final strides, Lewis edged ahead, raising his arm in victory as he hit the finish. He had clocked a record 9.86, with Burrell at 9.88, and four others under 10 seconds.

"To be 30 years old and to get my first true world record on the track really means something to me," exclaimed Lewis.

## FINAL RESULTS (8/25)
1. Carl Lewis (USA).............................................. 9.86 world record
2. Leroy Burrell (USA) ........................................ 9.88
3. Dennis Mitchell (USA)..................................... 9.91
4. Linford Christie (Great Britain) ....................... 9.92
5. Frank Fredericks (Namibia) ............................ 9.95
6. Ray Stewart (Jamaica) .................................... 9.96
7. Robson da Silva (Brazil) ................................. 10.12
8. Bruny Surin (Canada) ..................................... 10.14

# No. 73 -- Pac-8 Men's Cross Country, Stanford 1969: Lindgren vs. Prefontaine

In the fall of 1969, two of the giants of American distance running faced off. Washington State's Gerry Lindgren had already won two NCAA cross country titles, had run a world record, and competed in the Olympics. Steve Prefontaine, Oregon's sensational frosh, had upset Lindgren two weeks earlier.

When the gun went off, the two sprinted away as the rest of the strong field chased behind in awe. Eventually they had 200 yards on the field, fighting each other for the lead in a see-saw battle that never saw one get more than an arm's-length ahead of the other.

They crossed the finish line in a tangle, Lindgren getting the nod as many observers felt the outcome was too close to call. Both clocked 28:32.4 for the six-mile trek across the Stanford Golf Course. "I was going all out," Prefontaine told *Track & Field News's* Jon Hendershott. "We didn't plan to tie. I felt I had to go fast from the start because Gerry is fast."

Said Lindgren, "I planned to go after Steve and stay with him at first. I wanted to go by him and leave him several times but I couldn't."

Nine days later, Lindgren "ran scared" to lead the NCAA final from start to finish. Pre finished third behind Mike Ryan of Air Force, but would go on to win three NCAA harrier titles of his own.

## FINAL RESULTS (11/15)

| | |
|---|---|
| 1. Gerry Lindgren (Washington St) | 28:32.4 |
| 2. Steve Prefontaine (Oregon) | 28:32.4 |
| 3. Steve Savage (Oregon) | 28:58 |
| 4. Rick Riley (Washington St) | 29:02 |
| 5. Greg Brock (Stanford) | 29:08 |
| 6. Mark Hiefield (Washington St) | 29:10 |
| 7. Fred Ritcherson (Southern California) | 29:11 |
| 8. Jeff Marsee (Southern California) | 29:12 |

# No. 72 -- London vs Moscow 5,000, London 1954: Chataway vs. Kuts

World record-holder Vladimir Kuts knew he would have a tough run against Britain's Chris Chataway, under the lights and in front of 50,000 of Chataway's countrymen. After a fast first mile of 4:24.4, Kuts began launching into his fabled surges of 60-second pace running. The first one caught Chataway off-guard, but after that he covered the Russian's moves well.

By the time the bell lap rang, the din of the crowd chanting Chataway's name had grown unbelievably loud. Kuts began his final surge, and tore past the three-mile mark in a world record 13:27.0. The Briton never flagged, and coming off the last turn he rose up on his toes and started sprinting. He caught Kuts with 10 yards to go and crossed the line just two feet ahead of the master.

The time, 13:51.6, was a world record, as Kuts, a tenth back, also bettered the old mark of 13:56.6 that he had set six weeks earlier. Coincidentally, Chataway had run his last lap in 60.1, the same split that friend Roger Bannister had used earlier that year in finishing the first-ever four-minute mile. Stunned by the defeat, Moscow radio abruptly ceased its coverage of the event. Ten days later, Kuts ran 13:51.2 to regain his record.

## FINAL RESULTS (10/13)
1. Chris Chataway (Great Britain) ......................... 13:51.6 world record
2. Vladimir Kuts (Soviet Union) ............................ 13:51.7
3. Peter Driver (Great Britain) .............................. 14:29.2
4. Vladimir Okorokov (Soviet Union)...................... 14:50.0

# No. 71 -- Olympic Men's 400, Seoul 1988: Lewis vs. Reynolds

Olympic Trials winner Butch Reynolds had just set the world record of 43.29. Danny Everett had placed second at the Trials in 43.98. The third member of the U.S. 400 squad was 19-year-old Steve Lewis, considered to be a great prospect, but not ready for gold.

Everett, Lewis's UCLA teammate, took the pace out hard, but by 200 (21.37), Lewis had pulled nearly even. Reynolds, playing it too safe, ran far behind. At 300, Lewis had edged into the lead, while Reynolds began his trademark stretch drive.

Spectators cheered and agonized as Reynolds charged past Everett and toward Lewis. He came oh-so-close to winning it all, but Lewis thwarted him by producing the best lean to win in 43.87. Reynolds finished 0.06 behind as the U.S. swept the medals.

Said Reynolds, "I got too confident. I had a lot left, but he was too far out to catch."

## FINAL RESULTS (9/28)

1. Steve Lewis (USA) ............................................................. 43.87
2. Butch Reynolds (USA) ..................................................... 43.93
3. Danny Everett (USA) ....................................................... 44.09
4. Darren Clark (Australia) ................................................. 44.55
5. Innocent Egbunike (Nigeria) ............................................ 44.72
6. Bert Camron (Jamaica) .................................................... 44.94
7. Ian Morris (Trinidad) ...................................................... 44.95
8. Mohamed Al-Malki (Oman) .............................................. 45.03

# No. 70 -- AAU Men's 100, Lincoln 1935: Owens vs. Peacock

The journalists of the time called it "the greatest 100-meter field ever." No wonder. Earlier that spring, Jesse Owens had broken four world records in the space of 45 minutes. Ralph Metcalfe, the defending champion and one of the event's all-time greats, joined him on the AAU starting line on July 4. So did the great Eulace Peacock, from Temple University. Among the challengers was George Anderson, a 9.4 (world record) performer for 100 yards.

Anderson led early, but Peacock started to pull away at the halfway point. Owens, still a year away from Olympic glory, charged into second. Then Metcalfe used his characteristically strong finishing drive to make things interesting. He passed Owens and just missed tagging Peacock at the line. Peacock had clocked 10.2, better than the world record, but wind-aided. It was a good day for the future Coast Guard man, who won the long jump as well, with the second longest jump in history, 26-feet, three inches (8.00).

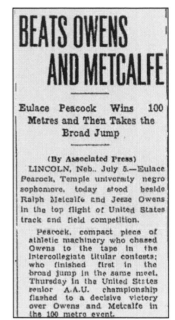

## BEATS OWENS AND METCALFE

Eulace Peacock Wins 100 Metres and Then Takes the Broad Jump

(By Associated Press)

LINCOLN, Neb., July 5.—Eulace Peacock, Temple university negro sophomore, today stood beside Ralph Metcalfe and Jesse Owens in the top flight of United States track and field competition.

Peacock, compact piece of athletic machinery who chased Owens to the tape in the intercollegiate titular contests; who finished first in the broad jump in the same meet, Thursday in the United States senior A.A.U. championship flashed to a decisive victory over Owens and Metcalfe in the 100 metre event.

*[The Leader Post · July 4, 1935]*

In later years, Peacock had a varied professional career. In addition to his Coast Guard stint, he worked as a New York City teacher, an IRS agent, and a liquor store owner. He was also a longtime track official. He died in 1996.

## FINAL RESULTS (7/4)
1. Eulace Peacock ...................... 10.2w
2. Ralph Metcalfe ...................... 10.3
3. Jesse Owens .......................... 10.3
4. George Anderson ................... 10.4
5. Foy Draper ............................ nt
6. Milton Holt ........................... nt

# No. 69 -- Italy vs Germany, Men's 800, Milan 1939: Harbig vs. Lanzi

In the late 1930s, the two finest half-milers in Europe were Mario Lanzi of Italy and Rudolf Harbig of Germany. Lanzi, who had won the silver in the 1936 Games behind American John Woodruff, regretted his passive tactics that day and transformed himself into a front-runner.

Harbig defeated Lanzi at the 1938 European Championships, and a fierce rivalry commenced. It finally came to a head at the Italy-Germany dual meet of 1939, with Europe already slipping into the Second World War.

Lanzi went out hard, 24.6, and Harbig content to run several meters back. At the 400, Lanzi clocked 52.5 to Harbig's 52.8. Both were well under world-record pace. Lanzi hit 600 in 1:19.8 with Harbig moving up on him, but at 700 meters, the Italian crumbled.

Harbig went by him with a ferocious sprint that he carried all the way to the line. Thanks to Lanzi's maniacal front-running, he clocked 1:46.6, a world record by 1.8 seconds, and the biggest reduction of the 800-meter record ever. A defeated Lanzi jogged in at 1:49.0, still a personal best. Harbig's world record lasted 16 years. He died in action on the Russian front in 1944, defending a bridge from a Soviet advance.

## FINAL RESULTS (7/15)
1. Rudolf Harbig (Germany) ...................... 1:46.6 world record
2. Mario Lanzi (Italy)................................. 1:49.0
3. Hans Brandscheit (Germany) ................ 1:50.3
4. Mario Bellini (Italy)............................... 1:52.6

# No. 68 -- Olympic Men's High Jump, Rome 1960: Shavlakadze vs. Thomas

John Thomas stood as the strongest of favorites on the eve of the 1960 Games. The first man to jump 7-feet (2.14) indoors, he broke the outdoor world record an amazing five times in the weeks leading up to Rome. His best, 7-3¾ (2.23), came in winning the Olympic Trials.

In Rome, however, Thomas was not prepared to see a challenge. As the competition wore on, "his mood changed from over-confidence to fear," wrote historian Roberto Quercetani. He began forgetting his warm-ups, and was clearly suffering from an attack of nerves. Three Russians began applying serious pressure. Thomas needed two tries to clear the ultimate height of 7-¼ (2.14), while Robert Shavlakadze (actually a Georgian) cleared it on his first for the gold.

Thomas ended up in a tie for the bronze, with the silver going (on misses) to Valeriy Brumel, who rose to much greater heights in coming years.

## FINAL RESULTS (9/1)
1. Robert Shavlakadze (Soviet Union) .................7-1          2.16
2. Valery Brumel (Soviet Union).........................7-1          2.16
3. John Thomas (USA)........................................7-¼        2.14
4. Viktor Bolshov (Soviet Union) ........................7-¼        2.14
5. Stig Pettersson (Sweden)...............................6-10¼      2.09
6. Charlie Dumas (USA) ....................................6-8          2.03
=7. Jiří Lanský (Czechoslovakia).........................6-8          2.03
=7. Kjell Åke Nilsson (Sweden) ..........................6-8          2.03
=7. Theo Püll (Germany) ...................................6-8          2.03

The three medalists at Rome.
[*PD-ITALIA*]

# No. 67 -- Olympic Men's 100, Los Angeles 1932: Tolan vs. Metcalfe

No closer call ever came in a men's Olympic dash final than the epic match between Ralph Metcalfe and Eddie Tolan. Metcalfe, the 5-foot-11 (1.80) Marquette star, towered over 5-4 (1.62) Michigan grad Eddie Tolan. On the track that season, Metcalfe had been equally dominant, never losing to anyone.

Fastest out of the holes (blocks were not widely used at the time) was Japan's Takayoshi Yoshioka, considered one of the greatest starters ever. He was still leading at 40 meters when Tolan pulled even. By 60 meters, Tolan had a clear lead, but Metcalfe began closing fast. The two came to the finish line together, with the rest of the field a yard back.

They crossed in a world record 10.3 (10.38 autotime, in one of the first meets to ever be so measured). Metcalfe's chest actually hit the line first, according to the photo. However, the rules of the time awarded the win to Tolan, because his torso cleared the finish before Metcalfe's did. Amazingly, before those results were even announced, the runners sensed how it would go. Tolan celebrated, while Metcalfe, later a U.S. congressman, "looked dejected," according to writer Wally Donovan.

Curiously, Tolan's mark was ratified as an equaling of the world record (first set in 1930 by Canadian Percy Williams). Metcalfe's mark was not recognized as a record.

## FINAL RESULTS (8/1)
1. Eddie Tolan (USA) ................................ 10.3 (10.38) =world record
2. Ralph Metcalfe (USA) ........................... 10.3 (10.38)
3. Arthur Jonath (Great Britain) .............. 10.4 (10.50)
4. George Simpson (USA) ......................... 10.5 (10.53)
5. Daniel Joubert (South Africa) ............... 10.6 (10.60)
6. Takayoshi Yoshioka (Japan) ................. 10.8 (10.79)

# No. 66 — Olympic Men's Pole Vault, Moscow 1980: Kazakiewicz vs. Volkov

Cordner Nelson of *Track & Field News* called it the "best competition" in pole vault history. It got serious when the bar went up to an Olympic record 18-2½ (5.55) with nine competitors left. Four made it, and three were eliminated.

At the next height (18-4½/5.60), two more cleared, including Poland's Wladyslaw Kozakiewicz, a failed favorite of the previous Olympics. The rest passed. Everyone jumped at 18-6½ (5.65), but only Kozakiewicz emerged with a perfect record. His three rivals -- Philippe Houvion, teammate Tadeusz Slusarski and the Soviet Union's Konstantin Volkov -- all needed three attempts.

At 18-8¼ (5.70), Houvion and Slusarski went out, while "Kozak" cleared on his first attempt. Volkov took two efforts, and passed his third. Kozak then faced 18-10¼ (5.75). The partisan Russian crowd began to whistle while he stood on the runway, in an attempt to spoil his jump. The announcer pleaded for quiet, to no avail. Kozak ignored the din, and soared over the bar. When he landed, he stood and defiantly flashed the crowd an obscene gesture.

When Volkov missed, the Pole had the gold, but he wasn't done. He had the bar raised to 18-11½ (5.78), a world record height. He cleared on his second try, and then put in three more attempts in the vain hope of becoming the first man to clear 19 feet (actually 19-1/5.82).

## FINAL RESULTS (7/30)

1. Wladyslaw Kozakiewicz (Poland) ............5.78    18-11½   world record
=2. Konstantin Volkov (Soviet Union) ..........5.65    18-6½
=2. Tadeusz Slusarski (Poland) ....................5.65    18-6½
4. Philippe Houvion (France)........................5.65    18-6½
5. Jean-Michel Bellot (France)......................5.60    18-4½
6. Mariusz Klimczyk (Poland)......................5.55    18-2½
7. Thierry Vigneron (France)........................5.45    17-10½
8. Sergey Kulibaba (Soviet Union)................5.45    17-10½

# No. 65 -- Olympic Women's 4 x 400, Seoul 1988: United States vs. Soviet Union

Figured to be a three-way matchup between the Soviets, East Germans and Americans, the Seoul relay turned out better than anyone had expected (except the East Germans). The U.S., keyed by Denean Howard's 49.82, got off to the early lead over the Soviets (50.12). On the second leg, Diane Dixon produced a sparkling 49.17, but was left in the wake of Olga Nazarova's 47.82.

Valerie Brisco brought the U.S. back into contention with her 48.44, as the Soviets managed only a 49.43, while the East Germans faded. The Soviets had a two-meter lead at the final hand-off, which set up a titanic confrontation between 400 winner Olga Bryzgina and triple gold medalist Florence Griffith Joyner.

Certainly, most Americans in the crowd expected Flojo to perform another miracle, even if she had just finished the 4 x 100 a half hour earlier. She got close, pulling to within a couple feet of the Russian. But Bryzgina had the best finish, and managed a 47.80 to hit the line in a world record 3:15.17. Flojo clocked 48.08, and brought the U.S. under the old best as well with a 3:15.51.

## FINAL RESULTS (10/1)

1. Soviet Union ................................. 3:15.17
(*T. Ledovskaya 50.12, O. Nazarova 47.82, M. Pinigina 49.43, O. Bryzgina 47.80*)
2. United States ............................... 3:15.51
(*D. Howard 49.82, D. Dixon 49.17, V. Brisco 48.44, F. Griffith Joyner 48.08*)
3. East Germany ............................... 3:18.29
4. West Germany ............................. 3:22.49
5. Jamaica ..................................... 3:23.13
6. Great Britain .............................. 3:26.89
7. France ....................................... 3:29.37
Canada ......................................... did not finish

# No. 64 -- Olympic Men's 10,000, Atlanta 1996: Gebrselassie vs. Tergat

For a long time, we saw Haile Gebrselassie as unbeatable. Back in 1996, however, many of us felt that the rest of the world had a chance. That is, until this race was over. The first half of the race was a ho-hum affair, the first five kilometers going by in 13:55.22. Then Kenyans Paul Koech and Josephat Machuka teamed up to push the field to world-record speeds.

Haile Gebrselassie [*Alexxx86*]

With six laps to go, Paul Tergat made his move. The lanky Kenyan was followed only by Gebrselassie, as the rest of the field burned away in the 60-second surge. With a lap to go, the Ethiopian blew past Tergat, and by the backstretch seemed to have victory assured.

But when he hit the homestretch, Gebrselassie looked back and inexplicably slowed, as Tergat came up with a powerful sprint.

The margin shrunk, but Geb held on for the win in an Olympic record 27:07.34, with Tergat clocking 27:08.17. The reason for the Ethiopian's fatigue became readily apparent when the realization hit that he had run the last half of the race in an astounding 13:11.4, faster than the winning time in every Olympic 5,000 but one.

## FINAL RESULTS (7/29)
1. Haile Gebreselassie (Ethiopia).............27:07.34
2. Paul Tergat (Kenya) ...........................27:08.17
3. Salah Hissou (Morocco)......................27:24.67
4. Aloys Nizigama (Burundi) ..................27:33.79
5. Josphat Machuka (Kenya)..................27:35.08
6. Paul Koech (Kenya) ...........................27:35.19
7. Khalid Skah (Morocco)........................27:46.98
8. Mathias Ntawulikura (Rwanda).........27:50.73

# No. 63 -- World Championships Women's 400 Hurdles, Gothenberg 1995: Batten vs. Buford

Many in the media dismissed this race because of the absence of stars such as world record-holder Sally Gunnell, Sandra Farmer-Patrick and Marie-Jose Perec. The lowered expectations amused Americans Kim Batten and Tonja Buford. "I knew Tonja would be tough to beat," said Batten, "and that I'd have to run fast."

Both decided to go out hard because of the windy conditions. Buford led early, but by the backstretch, Batten had command of the race. Illinois alum Buford started coming back over the last turn, then stuttered her steps at the ninth hurdle. She recovered well, and the two leaped the final hurdle together.

They sprinted to the finish nearly even, but Batten had the far better lean. She clocked a world record 52.61, with Buford a mere 0.01 behind, also under the old best. Batten, who had been hampered earlier in the year by an appendectomy and a toe problem, admitted, "At the line, I didn't know if I'd beat her."

## FINAL RESULTS (8/11)
1. Kim Batten (USA)....................................52.61 world record
2. Tonja Buford (USA) ...............................52.62
3. Deon Hemmings (Jamaica).......................53.48
4. Heike Meissner (Germany).......................54.86
5. Tatyana Tereshchuk (Ukraine).................54.94
6. Silvia Rieger (Germany) ...........................55.01
7. Ionela Tirlea (Romania)...........................55.46
8. Natalya Torshina (Kazakhstan)................56.75

# No. 62 -- World Championships Women's Heptathlon, Stuttgart 1993: Joyner-Kersee vs. Braun

Now that Jackie Joyner-Kersee is retired, it's easy to remember her as an all-conquering hero. The records show her dominance, but it was the occasional close call that showed her competitive nature.

A 12.89 in the hurdles put her in second. A disappointing 5-11¼ (1.81) high jump dropped her to third. Her speed came out at the end of the day, when her 23.10 in the 200 put her into the lead by 14 points. Her husband/coach Bob Kersee called it "her worst day."

A great 23-1¼ (7.04) in the long jump gave JJK a huge lead of 161 points, but the next event, the javelin, was one that usually caused her fans to cover their eyes in dread. JJK's 143-7 (43.76) put her more than 30 feet behind Germany's Sabine Braun, who took over the points lead. That meant that JJK had to run faster than Braun in the dreaded 800 meters in order to win. She took the challenge, running just ahead of the German until the final turn, when she blew her away to take the win, 6,837 points to 6,797.

"I really had to put it all together," said Joyner-Kersee.

## FINAL RESULTS (8/16–17)
1. Jackie Joyner-Kersee (USA) .......... 6837
2. Sabine Braun (Germany) ............... 6797
3. Svetlana Buraga (Belorus) ............. 6635
4. Svetla Dimitrova (Bulgaria) .......... 6508
5. Urszula Wlodarczyk (Poland) ........ 6394
6. Kym Carter (USA) ........................ 6357
7. Jane Flemming (Australia) ............ 6343
8. Birgit Clarius (Germany) .............. 6341

**Individual Breakdown:**

|       | 100H  | HJ         | SP            | 200   | LJ          | JT           | 800     |
|-------|-------|------------|---------------|-------|-------------|--------------|---------|
| JJK   | 12.89 | 1.81/5-11¼ | 14.38/47-2¼   | 23.19 | 7.04/23-1¼  | 43.76/143-7  | 2:14.49 |
| Braun | 13.25 | 1.90/6-2¾  | 14.62/47-11¾  | 24.12 | 6.54/21-5½  | 53.44/175-4  | 2:17.82 |

# No. 61 -- Boston Marathon 1982: Salazar vs. Beardsley

It would be the first Boston Marathon for both Alberto Salazar and Dick Beardsley. Salazar at the time was on top of the world. He had run a personal-best 10-kilometer run of 27:30 just nine days earlier, and was attempting to see if he could handle such a tough double in the 1984 Olympics.

Beardsley and Salazar had been together from the start of the race: "head-to-head from the time the gun went off," said Beardsley. By 18 miles, the rest of the field had dropped away and the Minnesota farmer started hammering the downhills in an attempt to drop Salazar.

"I was worried he might break me," said Salazar, who was also having problems with the heat.

With less than 800 meters left, the Oregon alum jumped into the lead. Beardsley tried to pass him back, and the two sprinted all the way to the finish, Salazar crossing in 2:08:51 to Beardsley's 2:08:53.

Said Salazar, "You go all that distance, so it would be crazy to let someone break you in the last few yards." It was the first time that two men broke 2:09 in the same race.

## FINAL RESULTS (4/19)
1. Alberto Salazar (Athletics West)...............2:08:51
2. Dick Beardsley (New Balance)..................2:08:53
3. John Lodwick (Athletics West)..................2:12:01
4. Bill Rodgers (Greater Boston) ...................2:12:13
5. Kjell-Erik Stahl (Sweden) .......................2:12:46
6. Dennis Rinde (West Virginia TC) .............2:15:04
7. Terry Baker (New Balance) ......................2:16:32
8. Rick Callison (Converse)...........................2:16:35

# No. 60 -- U.S. vs. Africa 10,000 Meters, Durham 1971: Yifter vs. Shorter

For Miruts Yifter and Frank Shorter, the first visit by an African track team to the United States resulted in a brutal clash. It gained even more drama from the previous day's 5,000-meter race between Ethiopian star Yifter and Steve Prefontaine.

Pre led most of the way in a moderate pace, passing two miles in 9 minutes and 1.2 seconds in 87-degree heat. Then with 700 yards to go, the 5-foot-6 Yifter exploded with a stunning kick. After a few steps, Pre decided to let him go. As it turns out, Yifter had miscounted laps, and after a blistering 57.6, he stopped with his arms raised. A befuddled Pre covered the real last lap in 70 seconds for the win.

The next day, 34,000 fans turned up in 91-degree heat, many of them cheering for Yifter. He stayed with Shorter until a lap to go, and then demonstrated his vicious kick again. This time he produced a 59.6 to win in 28:53.2 over five runners who had rested the previous day. Prefontaine told the TV cameras that Yifter's comeback was "fantastic."

Yifter would go on to win both events at the 1980 Olympics, a performance that another fabled Ethiopian star, Haile Gebrselassie, credits as his inspiration to start running.

## FINAL RESULTS (7/17)
1. Miruts Yifter (Ethiopia).......................28:53.2
2. Frank Shorter (USA)...........................28:54.0
3. Garry Bjorkland (USA)........................30:05.4
4. Wehib Masresha (Ethiopia)................30:34.4
5. Philip Ndoo (Kenya)...........................30:58.4

# No. 59. Olympic Men's 800, Los Angeles 1932: Hampson vs. Wilson

Considered to feature one of the strongest fields of the meet, the men's 800 lined up at a time when no man had yet broken the 1:50 barrier for two laps. NYU star Phil Edwards, a Canadian who had placed fourth in the previous Games, took the race out with a swift 24.4, 52.3 pace for the first lap. American Eddie Genung followed, as did Notre Dame star Alex Wilson, another Canadian.

Running fifth at the 400, British professor Tom Hampson clocked 54.8 and seemed no threat for a medal, let alone to Edwards, who had a lead of eight yards on the final turn. Then Genung narrowed that gap, with Wilson and Hampson also chasing. Wilson passed Genung and had soon moved past Edwards into the lead. Amazingly, Hampson kept coming, past Genung and Edwards. He moved even with Wilson and the two battled for each step.

At the line, Hampson prevailed by a foot. He (1:49.7) and Wilson (1:49.9) became the first men under 1:50. An early proponent of the values of even pacing, Hampson was hailed as one of the greatest middle distance runners of the time. He later added a silver medal in the 4 x 400 relay.

## FINAL RESULTS (8/2)

1. Tom Hampson (Great Britain) ......... 1:49.8 (1:49.70)   world record
2. Alex Wilson (Canada) ...................... 1:49.9
3. Phil Edwards (Canada) .................... 1:51.5
4. Eddie Genung (USA) ........................ 1:51.7
5. Edwin Turner (USA) ........................ 1:52.5
6. Chuck Honrbostel (USA) .................. 1:52.7
7. John Powell (Great Britain) ............. 1:53.1
8. Séraphim Martin (France) ............... 1:53.6

# No. 58 — World Championships Men's High Jump, Rome 1987: Sjoberg vs. Mogenburg

Bert Nelson called this "one of the greatest -- if not the greatest -- high jumping contests ever." Certainly, the quality of the field promised much: world record holder Patrik Sjöberg faced off against three former record holders, the defending champ, the Olympic gold medalist, as well as seven other men who had cleared 7-foot-8 that season.

At a meet record 7-7¼ (2.32), seven men cleared, while future great Javier Sotomayor went out on misses to finish ninth. At 7-8½ (2.35), Sjöberg and former record holder Dietmar Mögenburg cleared on their first tries; both had perfect records. Soviet Igor Paklin cleared on his second, and his teammate, Gennadiy Avdeyenko, made it on his third. Romanian Sorin Matei passed, leaving five in the quest for medals as the bar raised to 7-9¾ (2.38).

Sjöberg cleared on his first try, the only man to do so. Mögenburg decided to pass to the next height. The Soviets, however, reasoned that if they made 7-9¾ (2.38), they would win the remaining medals, should Mögenburg falter at 7-10¾ (2.41). Good call. Both Soviets cleared on their third attempts.

When the bar moved to 7-10¾ (2.41), only a half inch below the world record, no one had any luck, least of all Mögenburg. He ended up without any medal at all. Sjöberg, a Swede, came closest to clearing. Celebrating his gold medal, he called himself "lucky" anyway.

## FINAL RESULTS (9/6)

1. Patrik Sjöberg (Sweden) ............................. 2.38    7-9¾
=2. Igor Paklin (Soviet Union) ......................... 2.38    7-9¾
=2. Gennadiy Avdeyenko (Soviet Union) ......... 2.38    7-9¾
4. Dietmar Mögenburg (West Germany).......... 2.35    7-8½
5. Nick Saunders (Bermuda) ............................. 2.32    7-7¼
6. Sorin Matei (Romania) ................................. 2.32    7-7¼
7. Jan Zvara (Czechoslovakia) ......................... 2.32    7-7¼
8. Carlo Thranhardt (West Germany) ............. 2.29    7-6

# No. 57 -- Olympic Women's 10,000, Barcelona 1992: Tulu vs. Meyer

At the Worlds the previous year, Liz McColgan used a brutal pace to burn the competition away and win gold. Here, she tried it again, but a lot had changed in a year. Running even faster than she had in Tokyo, McColgan at 3,000m had 11 competitors bunched up behind her as if she were slowing down traffic.

Over the next few miles the pack thinned out a bit, but McColgan's fate was sealed when South African Elana Meyer tore into the lead with less than 10 laps to go.
Only Ethiopian Derartu Tulu could follow her, refusing to take the lead even when Meyer swung wide to grab wet sponges. When the final bell rang, Tulu blasted past Meyer and built a 5.73-second margin on the final lap, finishing in 31:06.02, an African record and a time only four women had ever bettered. McColgan placed fifth.

The two Africans joined in an embrace and a memorable victory lap. Tulu had won the first medal ever by an Ethiopian woman, while Meyer had captured the first medal for the South African team, welcomed back into the Olympics after three decades away.

## FINAL RESULTS (8/7)
1. Derartu Tulu (Ethiopia)............................ 31:06.02
2. Elana Meyer (South Africa) ...................... 31:11.75
3. Lynn Jennings (USA)................................ 31:19.89
4. Zhong Huandi (China) .............................. 31:21.08
5. Liz McColgan (Great Britain) ................... 31:26.11
6. Wang Xiuting (China).............................. 31:28.06
7. Uta Pippig (Germany)............................. 31:36.45
8. Judi St. Hilaire (USA).............................. 31:38.04

# No. 56 -- Olympic Women's High Jump, Seoul 1988: Ritter vs. Kostadinova

Amid the glitter of FloJo and her world records, and the controversy over Ben Johnson, one of the biggest stories of the Seoul Olympics has been all but forgotten. Texan Louise Ritter might have had a chance against Bulgaria's Stefka Kostadinova, but not much of one.

Kostadinova, after all, had leaped over 6-8 (2.03) a total of 29 times. Ritter had done it once; it was her American record. Kostadinova, in the five seasons leading up to their Olympic encounter, had won 72 of her 75 competitions, and owned the world record of 6-10¼ (2.09). Big, big favorite.

For the Bulgarian, everything went as expected as the bar climbed to 6-7 (2.01). She never missed, and her competitors dropped away one by one. All except for Ritter, who was also jumping perfectly. When the bar went to 6-8 (2.03), they were the only ones left. Ritter's fans were probably overjoyed about her getting the silver; it's doubtful that even they anticipated that the unthinkable would happen.

But it did. First Kostadinova missed at 6-8 (2.03). Then Ritter did. Then Kostadinova missed again, as Ritter did. Then they both missed yet again. The tie had to be broken, so the officials instructed them both to try 6-8 (2.03) one more time, the first Olympic jump-off since 1936. Kostadinova missed. Ritter cleared.

The Texan went wild in celebration. Later she said, "I still consider her the best high jumper in the world." Ritter could afford to be generous; she had the gold.

## FINAL RESULTS (9/30)
1. Louise Ritter (USA) .............................6-8     2.03
2. Stefka Kostadinova (Bulgaria).............6-7     2.01
3. Tamara Bykova (Soviet Union)...........6-6¼   1.99
4. Olga Turchak (Soviet Union)...............6-5     1.96
=5. Galina Astafei (Romania) ..................6-4     1.93
=5. Lyudmila Andonova (Bulgaria) .........6-4     1.93
7. Christine Stanton (Australia)..............6-4     1.93
8. Diana Davies (Great Britain)..............6-2¾   1.90

# No. 55 -- European Champs 10,000, Helsinki 1971: Vaatainen vs. Bedford

Britain's Dave Bedford had run the second-fastest time in history earlier that season, a 27:47.0 that marked him as the man to beat. He ran from the front, knowing his only hope for gold was to burn off the kickers. Among his pursuers were two Finns, Seppo Tuominen and Juha Vaatainen. That gave the nearly 40,000 Finns in the stadium something to cheer about.

After halfway, reached in a blistering 13:54.4, the two Finns shook up the race with hard surges. Bedford fell back for a while, but worked himself into the lead again a few laps later. The pack of six ran together until the bell. Bedford knew what kind of bad news that was for him. Sprinting as fast as he could, he watched as his five rivals blew past him on the last lap.

The most feared, East German Jurgen Haase, unleashed his stinging kick with 300 to go. However, he couldn't shake Vaatainen, who ran the whole distance with spike wounds in both legs. The Finn, a converted sprinter with a 400 best of 48.9, unleashed a 53.8 last lap, unheard of in 10,000 running. He demolished the East German to win in 27:52.8 as an unprecedented five men broke 28 minutes. Four days later, the expatriate Finn (he lived in Brazil), unleashed a similar kick to win the 5,000 gold.

## FINAL RESULTS (8/10)

1. Juha Väätäinen (Finland) .................................... 27:52.8
2. Jürgen Haase (East Germany) ........................... 27:53.4
3. Rashid Sharafyetdinov (Soviet Union) ................ 27:56.4
4. Dane Korica (Yugoslavia) ................................... 27:58.4
5. Mariano Haro (Spain) ....................................... 27:59.4
6. Dave Bedford (Great Britain) ........................... 28:04.4
7. Mike Tagg (Great Britain) ................................ 28:14.8
8. Seppo Tuominen (Finland) ................................ 28:18.0

# No. 54 -- World Championships Men's Pole Vault, Tokyo 1991: Bubka vs. Bagyula

Over the years, Sergei Bubka has won many competitions, six world titles among them. The Ukrainian, however, would be hard-pressed to come up with a greater victory than his third gold in the Worlds. Bubka had a bad heel bruise that had been troubling him for a month. Ninety minutes before the competition, he had gotten injections of a pain-killer. His other heel hurt him as well, but he decided not to get shots in both.

The ailing world record holder's strategy was simple: Don't jump unless absolutely necessary. His competitors took their attempts at the lower heights while he watched. He finally stepped on the runway when the bar hit 18-8¼ (5.70). He cleared easily, but limped away. "The pain was so severe ... I started to get concerned," he said.

He had a doctor give him another injection. Then he stepped up for his second jump of the day, with the bar at 19-4¼ (5.90). Favoring his heel, he put too much stress on his left arch, straining a muscle. He crashed into the bar. The next jumper, Hungarian István Bagyula (an NCAA champ from George Mason), cleared the height, moving into the lead.

Bubka decided to save his last two attempts for 19-6¼ (5.95), a height Bagyula had never reached. Shortening his run-up, he blew his first try. Bagyula did as well, and Russian Maksim Tarasov closed out his day with a miss. Then the Great One stepped up for his final leap. If he made it, he would win. If he missed, he would earn a humbling sixth-place: "I was desperate."

He banished the pain from his mind, and ran down the runway at full speed. He soared far above the bar in one of the greatest leaps of his career, capturing the gold with his second clearance of the day. Said an amazed Bagyula, "We can only dream about first place; he is so much better than us."

## FINAL RESULTS (8/29)

1. Sergey Bubka (Soviet Union)............5.95    19-6¼
2. István Bagyula (Hungary)................5.90    19-4¼
3. Maksim Tarasov (Soviet Union)........5.85    19-2¼
4. Radio Gataullin (Soviet Union)..........5.85    19-2¼
5. Peter Widén (Sweden).......................5.75    18-10¼
6. Tim Bright (USA).............................5.75    18-10¼
7. Hermann Fehringer (Austria)..........5.60    18-4½
8. Thierry Vigneron (France)................5.60    18-4½

# No. 53 -- Olympic Women's 3,000, Los Angeles 1984: Slaney vs. Budd

In the hype-driven L.A. Olympics, few competitions generated as much frenzy beforehand as the eagerly anticipated clash between Mary Slaney and Zola Budd. Slaney, America's dominant distance runner, had captured a stirring 1,500/3,000 double at the previous year's World Championships. Budd, a waif-like South African with a penchant for running dazzling times barefoot, had gotten around the international embargo on athletes from her country by going through the express line to get British citizenship.

Slaney took off at a fast pace, hoping for an 8:30. When the pace slowed, Budd tried to run to the front. Her teammate, Wendy Sly, also moved. Sly came alongside Slaney at the mile, but Budd managed to shoot between them and take the lead. Running hard, she pulled Slaney, Sly, and Maricica Puica away from the pack.

However, both Slaney and Budd were vastly inexperienced at running in a crowd, and it showed. The two bumped twice, and at 1,720m, Slaney went down. She injured her hip, and could not get up. Budd continued to race, but the booing of the boorish crowd rattled her. The 18-year-old was clearly finished when Puica and Sly went past her with little more than a lap to go.

Puica outkicked Sly for the gold, 8:35.96 to 8:39.47, enshrining herself as the answer to the trivia question, Who won the Slaney-Budd matchup?

Slaney, after her bitter post-race outbursts at Budd, later reconciled with her and eventually laid the blame on her own inexperience at running in packs. Her best year came in 1985, when she went on a tear in Europe, winning 12 major races and breaking the world mile record with a 4:16.71. Budd went back to London to face the same harassment and death threats that had started when she accepted a British passport. Though she also had a great campaign the next year, she would retire from the sport long before reaching her potential.

## FINAL RESULTS (8/10)
1. Maricica Puică (Romania).................8:35.96
2. Wendy Sly (Great Britain)................8:39.47
3. Lynn Williams (Canada)...................8:42.14
4. Cindy Bremser (USA) .....................8:42.78
5. Cornelia Bürki (Switzerland)............8:45.20
6. Aurora Cunha (Portugal).................8:46.37
7. Zola Budd (Great Britain)................8:48.80
8. Joan Hansen (USA) .......................8:51.53

# No. 52 — Olympic Men's Triple Jump, Mexico City 1968: Saneyev tops World Record Binge

Even if you weren't alive yet in 1968, the event you remember most from the Mexico City Olympics is certainly Bob Beamon's historic long jump. The day before, however, the triple jump served notice that the something was special, and perhaps even askew, about the competition in the Estadio Olimpico.

Giuseppe Gentile of Italy started the fireworks in the qualifying round. A 53-foot (16.15+) jumper, he flew out to 56-1¼ (17.10) for a new world record. Then, in the finals, Gentile produced another world record, this time a 56-6 (17.22). Gold medal territory? No way.

In round three, the Soviet Union's Viktor Saneyev tacked a quarter-inch onto the world record, his 56-6¼(17.23) taking the lead. Two rounds later, Nelson Prudencio of Brazil broke the world record with a 56-8 (17.27). On the final round, Saneyev mounted an impressive run and bounced out to 57-¾ (17.39) to grab the gold for good. For sheer excitement, no other triple jump contest had ever hit this level.

The world record going in was only 55-10½ (17.03), a mark that would not have finished in the top five. What caused the orgy of great jumping? Thin air. In 1968, few realized what effect altitude had in allowing greater sprint/jump performances. Others have also pointed to the synthetic track, the first ever used for an Olympics.

Unfortunately, the evidence also points to misuse of the wind gauge by officials perhaps too eager to see world records. All of the world-record marks in Mexico City came with "legal" wind, but a suspicious five of 12 came with the wind exactly at the maximum allowable reading of 2.0 meters per second. None registered beyond that. Venerable track historian Roberto Quercetani was being generous when he called it a "stupendous" coincidence.

## FINAL RESULTS (10/17)

| | | | |
|---|---|---|---|
| 1. Viktor Saneyev (Soviet Union) | 17.39 | 57-¾ | world record |
| 2. Nelson Prudencio (Brazil) | 17.27 | 56-8 | |
| 3. Giuseppe Gentile (Italy) | 17.22 | 56-8½ | |
| 4. Art Walker (USA) | 17.12 | 56-2 | |
| 5. Nikolay Dudin (Soviet Union) | 17.09 | 56-1 | |
| 6. Phil May (Australia) | 17.02 | 55-10¼ | |
| 7. József Schmidt (Poland) | 16.89 | 55-5 | |
| 8. Mansour Dia (Senegal) | 16.73 | 54-10¾ | |

# No. 51 -- Olympic Trials Men's 400, Eugene 1972: Collett vs. Evans

Longtime observer of the sport Bob Hersh sums up the Trials 400 of 1972 with one word: "Wow!" The field was dazzling: Maurice Peoples, Curtis Mills, John Smith, Tommie Turner, Vince Matthews, Lee Evans, Fred Newhouse and Wayne Collett. Newhouse had blazed a 44.2 to win his semi. Collett won the other, in 44.8.

In the final, Newhouse ran like a crazy man. He hit the 200 fast, somewhere in the 20.3-20.7 range. Smith and Collett followed. Evans, the world record holder, trailed in fifth. Newhouse started to tie up on the last turn, and the smooth Smith (now the coach of Maurice Greene, among others), floated past.

On the straight, his former UCLA teammate, Collett moved into the lead. Newhouse held onto third until Evans collared him near the finish. Collett crossed victorious in 44.1, the fastest-ever at low altitude. Smith, recovered from a serious bout of hepatitis seven months earlier, ran 44.3. "This really means something," said Collett of his first major win.

## FINAL RESULTS (7/9)
1. Wayne Collett (Santa Clara Striders) ............... 44.1
2. John Smith (UCLA) ........................................... 44.3
3. Vince Matthews (BOHAA) ................................ 44.9
4. Lee Evans (Bay Area Striders) .......................... 45.1
5. Maurice Peoples (Arizona State) ....................... 45.3
6. Tommie Turner (Sports International) ............. 45.4
7. Fred Newhouse (U.S. Army) ............................ 45.4
8. Curtis Mills (Philadelphia Pioneer Club) .......... 45.4

# No. 50 -- World Championships Women's 4 x 100 Relay, Stuttgart 1993: The United States vs. Russia

A tremendous display of sprint talent highlighted one of the greatest one-lap relays ever. The U.S. team featured 200 silver medalist Gwen Torrence and seemingly unbeatable Gail Devers on anchor. They faced a solid Russian squad, anchored by Irina Privalova, and Jamaica, with 200 winner Merlene Ottey.

American Michelle Finn ran a decent first leg, but struggled to get the baton to Torrence. They lost ground, but Torrence made it up quickly, and handed off to Wenda Vereen. A rookie at this level, Vereen could barely keep even with Russian Natalya Voronova's storming leg. At the hand-off, the Russians and Americans were even.

Devers ran calm and controlled, moving slightly ahead of Privalova. The Russian frantically fought to get that edge back, and started her lean before Devers. She claimed she ran the last 20 meters with her eyes closed. At the line, the two teams seemed inseparable. They both ran the same time, 41.49, national records for the U.S. and Russia, and the second-fastest time ever. The Russians, however, got the gold.

## FINAL RESULTS (8/22)
1. Russia.................................... 41.49
(Olga Bogoslovskaya, Galina Malchugina, Natalya Voronova, Irina Privalova 9.89)
2. United States....................................... 41.49 American record
(Michelle Finn, Gwen Torrence, Wendy Vereen, Gail Devers 9.86)
3. Jamaica .............................................. 41.94
(Michelle Freeman, Juliet Campbell, Nikole Mitchell, Merlene Ottey)
4. France................................... 42.67
5. Germany............................... 42.79
6. Cuba ................................... 42.89
7. Finland ............................... 43.37
8. Great Britain....................... 43.86

Arnold Jackson sprinting to victory over Abel Kiviat in the
1912 Olympic 1500m final. [*1912 Official Olympic Report*]

Otis Davis outleans Carl Kaufmann to win
the 1960 Olympic 400m gold.

Jesse Owens at the 1936 Olympics [*Die Olympischen Spiele, 1936*]

Rudolf Harbig winning the epic battle against Italy's Mario Lanzi
over 800m. The resulting world record would last 16 years.
[*HistoriaAtletismo*]

Emil Zátopek, winner of four Olympic gold medals in distance running. [*Deutsche Fotothek*]

# No. 49 -- International Freedom Games Mile, Kingston 1975: Bayi vs. Liquori

After the 1974 Commonwealth Games, Filbert Bayi's front-running came as no surprise. When he passed the first lap in 56.9, no one went with him. Ireland's Eamonn Coghlan led the others at 58.9.

At halfway in 1:56.6, Bayi looked back to see where everybody was. All he saw were Coghlan and American star Marty Liquori running a 1:58. On the third lap, Bayi put on the brakes, and Coghlan and Liquori cut the gap. Liquori said, "Let's get him," but Coghlan apparently refused. With a lap to go, Coghlan finally moved up and passed Bayi on the inside.

The Tanzanian smoothly retook the lead, and then poured it on. "I knew it would take something out of them when they tried to pass me and couldn't," he said. Villanova alums Coghlan and Liquori battled for the second position, banging elbows on the turn, but neither was able to challenge Bayi.

He crossed the line in 3:51.0, breaking Jim Ryun's world record by a tenth of a second. Liquori ran a lifetime best of 3:52.2, and Coghlan 3:53.3 for a European record. Rick Wohlhuter ran 3:53.8 in fourth for his best time ever. It was the deepest mile race in history at that time.

## FINAL RESULTS (5/17)
1. Filbert Bayi (Tanzania) ............................ 3:51.0 world record
2. Marty Liquori (USA) ................................. 3:52.2
3. Eamonn Coghlan (Ireland) ........................ 3:53.3
4. Rick Wohlhuter (USA) .............................. 3:53.8
5. Tony Waldrop (USA) ................................. 3:57.7
6. Reggie McAfee (USA) ............................... 3:59.5
7. Walter Wilkinson (Great Britain) .............. 4:06.2
8. Sylvanus Barrett (Jamaica) ...................... nt

# No. 48 -- Olympic Trials Shot Put, Stanford 1960: Long vs. Nieder

The two men who had set world records that spring, Dallas Long and Bill Nieder, both figured to be among the top three. For the first two rounds, it looked like they would get their wish. Nieder struggled, however, and after the second round, the competition changed dramatically.

That's when Dave Davis showed up. He barely made it to the stadium at all, paying $18 to have a seaplane fly him 45 miles to the Palo Alto Harbor, then hitching a ride with a city employee to the stadium, changing his clothes in the car. Officials decided to allow him all six of his throws, and he proceeded to knock Nieder off the team with his fourth throw (62-3½/18.98). On his next throw, Nieder might have moved to second, but it was called foul, and he ended up in fourth place while Long took the win with a 63-3¾ (19.29).

Ironically, Davis injured his wrist afterwards, rendering his seaplane rescue for naught. In his place, Nieder was named to the Rome Olympic team, and won the gold with a throw of 64-6¾ (19.68).

## FINAL RESULTS (7/1)
1. Dallas Long (USC) ........................................ 19.30     63-3¾
2. Parry O'Brien (Santa Clara Striders) .......... 18.99     62-3¾
3. Dave Davis (Santa Clara Striders) .............. 18.98     62-3½
4. Bill Nieder (U.S. Army) ............................... 18.84     61-9¾
5. Jerry Winters (Stanford)............................. 18.26     59-11¼
6. Mike Lewis (Occidental) ............................. 17.19     56-4¾
7. Ken Bantum (New York PC)........................ 16.84     55-3
8. Glen Johnson (Santa Clara Striders) .......... 16.69     54-9

# No. 47 -- AAU Mile, San Diego 1965: Ryun vs. Snell

The Olympic champion against a high school kid. Who are you going to pick? Peter Snell, after winning two Olympic golds the previous fall, came to America to race. He had won a 3:56.4 contest in Compton, topping, among others, Jim Ryun at 3:56.8. Ryun had just graduated from Wichita East High School in Kansas, and he was too young to realize he was supposed to lose to a stud like Snell.

Three weeks later, at nationals, both Snell and Ryun ran conservatively, as Cary Weisiger took them through the half in 1:59.7. With 600 left, Czech Josef Odlozil took the lead, and the tension grew. Finally, with 300 left, Ryun took off. He felt so much power that he actually held back a bit: "It scared me to death." He waited for Snell to come, but instead it was Jim Grelle who pushed him on the last turn. Ryun beat him off, and when Snell finally came calling on the homestretch, Ryun had no problem staying ahead.

Jim Ryun [*University of Kansas*]

He crossed the line in 3:55.3, an American record, with a last lap in an unprecedented 53.9. Said Snell, "Ryun's got it."

## FINAL RESULTS (6/27)

1. Jim Ryun ..............................................3:55.3   American record
2. Peter Snell (New Zealand) ..................3:55.4
3. Jim Grelle ...........................................3:55.5
4. Josef Odlozil (Czechoslovakia) ...........3:57.7
5. Cary Weisiger ....................................4:04.9
6. Harry McCalla ...................................4:05.7

# No. 46 -- World Championships Men's Javelin, Rome 1987: Räty vs. Yevsyukov

No other nation has a javelin tradition like the Finns. While it's not a guarantee that the Finns will always win the gold, sometimes it seems that way. Take Seppo Räty. He wasn't even that good: added to the Finnish team at the last minute, not in the top 15 going into the meet, and only 10th after the qualifying round. Ho-hum stuff.

In the third round, however, the Finn popped a throw of 270-1, and took the lead away from Czech world record holder Jan Zelezny (269-8). Soviet Viktor Yevsyukov, a more likely winner than Raty, made things right in the fifth round by throwing a 270-9 to relegate Räty to silver. Then the 25-year-old Räty stepped up for his last throw and produced a 274-1, one of the best throws in history, to seal his upset.

Räty won silver in 1992 and bronze in 1996. He now coaches other Finnish javelin throwers.

## FINAL RESULTS (8/30)
1. Seppo Räty (Finland) .................................83.54      274-1
2. Viktor Yevsyukov (Soviet Union) ..............82.52      270-9
3. Jan Zelezny (Czechoslovakia) ..................82.20      269-8
4. Tom Petranoff (USA) ..............................81.28      266-8
5. Lev Shatilo (Soviet Union) .......................81.02      265-9
6. Kazuhiro Mizoguchi (Japan) ....................80.24      263-3
7. Mick Hill (Great Britain) .........................79.66      261-4
8. Dag Wennlund (Sweden) ........................78.40      257-3

# No. 45 -- World Cup Women's 400, Düsseldorf 1977: Szewinska vs. Koch

Irina Szewinska of Poland was already a legend when she stepped onto the track that day: world record holder, six Olympic medals. Her challenger, East German Marita Koch, would soon enough become a world-beater. In fact, she had beaten the Pole in a 200 earlier that season, and just two days before had outrun her on a 4 x 400 anchor, 49.3 to 49.9.

In this classic generational clash, Koch, running from lane 4, knew she had to build a big lead to overcome Szewinska's famous finish. The Pole ran from behind, in lane 5. At 300 meters, Koch had nearly a four-meter gap. It wasn't enough. Szewinska, 31, unleashed her long stride and ran the 20-year-old Koch down, passing her with 25 meters left to claim the win, 49.52 to 49.76. Said Koch, "As soon as I felt her beside me, I knew I was beaten."

In the coming years, Koch lowered the 400 best seven times, finally reaching 47.60, a mark that has never been approached.

## FINAL RESULTS (9/3)
1. Irina Szewinska (Poland).....................49.52
2. Marita Koch (East Germany)..............49.76
3. Marina Sidorova (Soviet Union) ..........51.29
4. Sharon Dabney (USA) ........................51.96
5. Aurelia Pentón (Cuba) ........................52.33
6. Verna Burnard (Australia) .................52.57
7. Ruth Waithira (Kenya) .......................53.90
8. Than Than (Burma)............................55.88

# No. 44 -- Olympic Men's 800, Munich 1972: Wottle vs. Arzhanov

Dave Wottle always thought he was a better 1,500-meter runner than a half-miler. Then came the Olympic Trials, where he cut three seconds off his best to tie the 800 world record. At the Olympics, Wottle tried again in the 1,500, but failed to make the final.

An Achilles injury after the Trials had led to some bad races before Munich. Soviet Yevgeniy Arzhanov looked to be the anointed one in the final. He led a hard-paced race, and in the last 200, his only rivals appeared to be Kenyans Robert Ouko and Mike Boit. The latter chased Arzhanov to the line, with the crowd erupting when it noticed Wottle sprinting madly from the back of the pack.

As the Soviet dove toward the line, Wottle edged past in the final step to win in 1:45.86. Said Arzanhov, "It is very disappointing to lose in the last stride by the length of your nose."

## FINAL RESULTS (9/2)
1. Dave Wottle (USA)..................................... 1:45.86
2. Yevgeniy Arzhanov (Soviet Union) ............ 1:45.89
3. Mike Boit (Kenya)..................................... 1:46.01
4. Franz-Josef Kemper (West Germany)........ 1:46.50
5. Robert Ouko (Kenya) ................................ 1:46.53
6. Andy Carter (Great Britain) ...................... 1:46.55
7. Andrzej Kupczyk (Poland) ........................ 1:47.10
8. Dieter Fromm (East Germany) .................. 1:47.96

# No. 43 -- USA Championships Men's Long Jump, New York 1991: Lewis vs. Powell

Carl Lewis, with 64 straight wins in the long jump, jumped 27-2½ (8.29) on his first leap and might have expected to win with that. Mike Powell, the next jumper, produced a 28-1¾ (8.58) that made Lewis take notice. In the next round, the Great One passed Powell with a 28-2¼ (8.59), thanking the crowd with a great flourish.

Not so fast, buddy. Powell boomed a 28-3¾ (8.63) to put the pressure back on. Lewis had not jumped that far in three years. He improved to 28-2¾ (8.60), which wasn't enough. Powell then jumped 27-10 (8.48). In the fourth round, Lewis managed a 27-9¼ (8.46) while Powell fouled. In round five, a worried Lewis could only go 28-¼ (8.54). Powell, on the brink of victory, passed.

With one last chance, Lewis summoned all his energies and flew out to 28-4¼ (8.64) to regain the lead. Powell, the wind out of his sails, could only respond with a 27-11½ (8.52). Behind Powell, Larry Myricks jumped 27-10¾ (8.50) and Llewellyn Starks hit 27-4 (8.33) for the best fourth-place jump ever. Win No. 65 for Lewis, but it served notice that his win streak was mortal.

## FINAL RESULTS (6/15)

1. Carl Lewis (Santa Monica TC)...............28-4¼          8.64
*(8.29/27-2½w, 8.59/28-2¼, 8.60/ 28-2¾, 8.46/27-9¼, 8.54/28-¼, 8.64/28-4¼)*
2. Mike Powell (Footlocker TC)...................28-3¾          8.63
*(8.58/28-1¾, 8.63/28-3¾, 8.48/27-10, foul, pass, 8.52/27-11½)*
3. Larry Myricks (Goldwin TC)...................27-10¾          8.50
4. Llewellyn Starks (STC) ..........................27-4½          8.34
5. Vernon George (unattached)...................26-6¼w          8.08
6. Keith Talley (DJE)................................26-1½          7.96
7. Russell Adams (unattached)...................26-1          7.95
8. Alan Turner (Indiana) ..........................25-11          7.90

# No. 42 — Olympic Javelin, Mexico City 1968: Lusis from Behind

Soviet great Janis Lusis (a Latvian) had every expectation of winning the Olympic gold. He had lorded over the world for six years and owned seven of the eight longest throws in history. But when he realized he was in fourth place after the first few throws, it got interesting.

Lusis moved into the lead in the second round with his 283-3 (86.34), an Olympic record. Then in the fourth round, Hungary's Gergely Kulcsar surprised with a 285-7 (87.04). Lusis responded with a throw so bad that he intentionally fouled it so that it wouldn't be measured. On his last chance, however, he launched the spear perfectly. It arced through the sky and hit the grass at 295-7 (90.10), winning the gold.

Journalist Mel Watman asked Lusis if he was worried going into that final attempt. "Oh no," came the reply.

## FINAL RESULTS (10/16)

1. Janis Lusis (Soviet Union) .............................295-7    90.10
*(81.74/268-2, 86.34/283-3, 82.66/272-2, 84.40/276-11, f, 90.10/295-7)*
2. Jorma Kinnunen (Finland) .............................290-7    88.58
*(86.30/283-2, f, f, 79.00/259-2, 85.82/281-7, 88.58/290-7)*
3. Gergely Kulcsar (Hungary)............................285-7    87.06
*(83.10/272-8, f, 83.82/275-0, 87.06/285-7, 85.14/279-4, 83.40/273-7)*
4. Wladislaw Nikiciuk (Poland) .........................281-2    85.70
5. Manfred Stolle (East Germany) .....................277-0    84.42
6. Karl-Ake Nilsson (Sweden)...........................273-11   83.48
7. Janusz Sidlo (Poland) ...................................264-4    80.58
8. Urs von Wartburg (Switzerland)...................264-4    80.56

# No. 41 -- AAU 100, Sacramento 1968: Hines vs. Greene

Richard Hymans called it "the greatest feast of 100-meter sprinting ever seen." Even though it came back in the days of hand-timing, when records were to be had relatively cheaply, it still stunned. The record at the time, 10.0, lay in tatters when the weekend was over.

In the heats, Jim Hines started the fireworks by producing a wind-aided 9.8, the fastest clocking ever. Lennox Miller ran his heat in 9.9 (windy). Then Charlie Greene (and Roger Bambuck behind him) caught a legal wind to tie the world record at 10.0. No less than 12 men now owned the record. With the wind noticeably stiller, Hines ripped the first semi in the first legal sub-10. In second, Ray Smith also hit 9.9 officially. The next semi saw Greene run another 9.9 world record, edging Miller and Bambuck.

One of the greatest fields ever lined up for the eagerly awaited final. Mel Pender got out best, and led for the first 90 meters. Greene outstarted Hines and they both chased Pender, catching him in the final strides. Amazingly, three others caught him as well, as the first seven all clocked 10.0, wind-aided.

The races had been auto-timed (unofficially) as well. Hines' semi actually was a 10.03, breaking Bob Hayes' auto 10.06 from the 1964 Olympics. Greene's semi took 10.10, and the final, 10.11w. Not bad for a dirt track.

## FINAL RESULTS (6/20)

1. Charlie Greene (USA)...................... 10.0w
2. Jim Hines (USA)............................. 10.0
3. Lennox Miller (Jamaica).................. 10.1
4. Roger Bambuck (France) ................ 10.1
5. Ronnie Ray Smith (USA) ................ 10.1
6. Mel Pender (USA)........................... 10.1

# No. 40 — Olympic Women's 4 x 400 Relay, Atlanta 1996: The United States vs. Nigeria

No certain gold was promised to the United States, and the team dug itself into a hole with a 51.68-second lead-off lap by Rochelle Stevens, who handed off in fourth place. Maicel Malone managed a 50.27 for the next circuit, passing the Nigerians to take the lead on the backstretch, only to be passed again by the Nigerians and Russians before the hand-off.

Kim Graham caught the Russian team on the backstretch and made up five meters on the Nigerians on the final turn. With the final exchange in sight, she took the lead, clocking 49.49 for her leg. She handed off to Jearl Miles, who jetted away with supreme confidence. What started to look like a certain win turned into a nail-biter as Nigeria's Fali Ogunkoya, the bronze medalist, ate up the lead and pulled nearly even on the homestretch.

Both women clawed to the finish and Miles prevailed, her 49.47 giving the U.S. a time of 3:20.91, just a step ahead of Nigeria's 3:21.04. Miles said the home track advantage paid off: "If it wasn't here in the USA, I would have gotten caught."

## FINAL RESULTS (8/3)

1. United States............................ 3:20.91
(R. Stevens 51.68, Maicel Malone 50.27, Kim Graham 49.49, Jearl Miles 49.47)
2. Nigeria....................................... 3:21.04
(Olabisi Afolabi 51.13, F. Yusuf 49.72, Charity Opara 51.29, F. Ogunkoya 49.80)
3. Germany.................................... 3:21.14
4. Jamaica ................................... 3:21.69
5. Russia....................................... 3:22.22
6. Cuba ........................................ 3:25.85
7. Czech Republic......................... 3:26.99
8. France....................................... 3:28.46

# No. 39 -- Olympic Men's 4 x 400, Tokyo 1964: The United States vs. Britain

U.S. coach Bob Giegengack had wanted Henry Carr to lead off the relay for the United States: "I told them they could run 2:58 with Carr leading off." The U.S. team, however, only wanted gold, and they knew that Carr could not be out-run on an anchor. They convinced the coach to do it their way.

So the best relay of the 1964 Games was led off by Ollan Cassell, who later became the head of USA Track and Field. Cassell split 46.0 to hand the baton off to Mike Larrabee just behind the British. Then Larrabee moved into the lead with a 44.8.

The third leg saw Ulis Williams run 45.4 to keep the U.S. just ahead of Trinidad. The last lap belonged to 200-meter winner Carr, who blistered a 44

.5 to bring the baton home in a world record 3:00.7. Britain's Robbie Brightwell closed well to give his team a 3:01.6 European record. Trinidad clocked 3:01.7, as all three medal winners dipped under the old world record of 3:02.2.

## FINAL RESULTS (10/21)
1. United States...................... 3:00.7   world record
*(Ollan Cassell 46.0, Mike Larrabee 44.8, Ulis Williams 45.4, Henry Carr 44.5)*
2. Great Britain...................... 3:01.6
*(Tim Graham 45.9, Adrian Metcalfe 45.5, John Cooper 45.4, R. Brightwell 44.8)*
3. Trinidad.............................. 3:01.7
4. Jamaica ............................. 3:02.3
5. Germany............................. 3:04.3
6. Poland ............................... 3:05.3
7. Soviet Union....................... 3:05.9
8. France................................ 3:07.4

# No. 38 -- Olympic Women's Long Jump, Moscow 1980: Kolpakova in Last-Round Flurry

When Soviet Tatyana Skachko leaped 22 feet, 10 inches (6.96) in the first round, she had reason to feel good about her chances; it was the seventh-best performance of all time. In the third round, she improved to 23-0 (7.01). Safer yet; no one had ever jumped that far and lost.

Then came the final round. Anna Wlodarczyk of Poland produced a 22-9¾ (6.95)to move into second. She celebrated wildly, thinking she might end up with silver. Then Soviet Tatyana Kolpakova flew to 23-2 (7.06) to capture gold. A jump later, East Germany's Brigitte Wujak produced a 23-1¼ (7.04) for silver.

Tom Jordan wrote in *Track and Field News*, "Skachko looked as if she had been struck by lightning. For more than an hour, she had been the gold medalist, and in the space of two minutes, she had gone from gold to silver to bronze. Wlodarczyk had gone from nothing to silver to nothing."

Said the winner, "One should always fight until the end."

## FINAL RESULTS (7/31)

1. Tatyana Kolpakova (Soviet Union) ..........7.06    23-2
2. Brigitte Wujak (East Germany) ...............7.04    23-1¼
3. Tatyana Skachko (Soviet Union) .............7.01    23-0
4. Anna Wlodarczyk (Poland)........................6.95    22-9¾
5. Siegrun Siegl (East Germany) .................6.87    22-6½
6. Jarmila Nygrýnová (Czechoslovakia)........6.83    22-5
7. Siegrid Heimann (East Germany)............6.71    22-¼
8. Lidiya Alfeyeva (Soviet Union) ................6.71    22-¼

# No. 37 — European Champs Women's High Jump, Prague 1978: Simeoni vs. Ackermann

Most felt that East Germany's Rosemarie Ackermann would, as usual, defeat Italian Sara Simeoni. It didn't matter that Simeoni had recently jumped a world-record 6-7 (2.01), or that Ackermann was nursing a sore ankle and heel.

The lead changed hands a total of seven times on the briskly cold day, with temperatures in the 50s. At 6-5½ (1.97), Ackermann took over from Simeoni (who had her first miss) as the rest of the field retired. Then, at 6-6¼ (1.99), it was Simeoni who made it on her first clearance, while Ackermann, a straddler, needed two tries. For each, it was the second time in their careers they had jumped that high.

The bar then moved to a world record-tying 6-7 (2.01). With a light rain falling, they both missed their first tries, but Simeoni cleared it on her second to claim the lead.

Ackermann, on her second try, also apparently cleared, but as she raised her hands in triumph, the bar fell off the standards. Said British track expert Richard Hymans, "Ackermann was a good winner and a very gracious loser. Simeoni had the demeanor and Italian star quality of a Diva."

## FINAL RESULTS (8/31)
1. Sara Simeoni (Italy)................................ 2.01    6-7   =world record
2. Rosemarie Ackermann (East Germany) . 1.99    6-6¼
3. Brigitte Holzapfel (West Germany) ........ 1.95    6-4¾
4. Jutta Kirst (East Germany).................... 1.93    6-4
5. Ulrike Meyfarth (West Germany).......... 1.91    6-3¼
6. Andrea Matay (Hungary) ...................... 1.85    6-¾
7. Snezana Hrepevnik (Yugoslavia)............ 1.85    6-¾
8. Urszula Kielan (Poland) ........................ 1.85    6-¾

# No. 36 — Olympic Men's 400 Hurdles, Seoul 1988: Phillips tops Moses

For years Andre Phillips had chased the unbeatable Edwin Moses. Countless times he had come up short. He planned his training, though, around the Olympic final, and when he pulled even with the world record holder halfway through the race, he knew he had more than a chance.

On the final turn, Phillips gradually pulled away. He strode down the straightaway powerfully. The expected charge from Moses never materialized. The surprise came from Senegal's Amadou Dia Ba, who had never broken 48 seconds before. The African, a converted high jumper, put on a tremendous burst and nearly caught Phillips at the line. Phillips won the gold in 47.19 to Dia Ba's 47.23. Moses settled for bronze.

Said Phillips of Moses, "He's been my motivation, my incentive, my idol."

## FINAL RESULTS (9/25)
1. Andre Phillips (USA) ...............................47.19
2. Amadou Dia Ba (Senegal) ........................47.23
3. Edwin Moses (USA) ...............................47.56
4. Kevin Young (USA)................................47.94
5. Winthrop Graham (Jamaica) ...................48.04
6. Kriss Akabusi (Great Britain)..................48.69
7. Harald Schmid (West Germany)..............48.76
8. Edgar Itt (West Germany) .......................48.78

# No. 35 -- Olympic Men's 5000m, Munich 1972: Viren Nails the Finish

Viren's second gold in Munich is perhaps the most talked-about, argued-about and written-about race in history. Certainly no other race--in the minds of American fans--has taken on so much drama, this being a key point in the plot development of the tragedy of Steve Prefontaine.

Perhaps the young American was doomed to lose this from the start. He never had an exceptional kick. While he railed often against the European and African veterans who relied on their finish, the elemental rule is that getting to the finish line first matters; how one gets there doesn't. Decades of tactical races since Prefontaine have only supported the theorem that in a slow race, the kicker will almost always triumph.

In Munich, the race dawdled. Pre's chances died in the first two miles (8:56.4). He played his only remaining card: the long drive. He took the lead and hit 62.5, 61.2, and 60.3. The field crumbled, except for four others: Emiel Puttemans, Ian Stewart, defender Mohamed Gamoudi, and Finn Lasse Viren, who won the 10,000 a few days earlier in a world record despite falling.

Viren floated into the lead with 300 left as Prefontaine sprinted. Gamoudi also went, and cut off Pre's momentum, moving ahead of Viren. Pre dropped back on the last turn, then rallied. It was too late. Viren easily loped away from Gamoudi, who in turn left Pre behind, to be picked off by Stewart. "I gave it everything I had and relied on my sprinting force," said Viren.

Prefontaine was conflicted after the race. On the one hand, he said, "I figured if I can't win in the last five laps, I'm not going to be the guinea pig the whole way." But he also said, "The pace wasn't fast enough. If it had been 8:40, I would have had gold or silver." He would probably have finished fifth had Miruts Yifter run. The Ethiopian --possibly the fastest kicker of the decade-- had won bronze in the 10,000. This day, he went to the wrong stadium gate and was not allowed in. As the race started, he cried alone in the tunnel.

## FINAL RESULTS (9/10)
1. Lasse Viren (Finland) ........................ 13:26.4
2. Mohamed Gamoudi (Tunisia) ............ 13:27.4
3. Ian Stewart (Great Britain) .............. 13:27.6
4. Steve Prefontaine (USA) ................... 13:28.4
5. Emiel Puttemans (Belgium) ............. 13:30.8
6. Harald Norpoth (West Germany) ...... 13:32.6
7. Per Halle (Norway) ........................... 13:34.6
8. Nikolay Sviridov (Soviet Union) ........ 13:39.4

# No. 34 -- European Championships Men's 10,000, Prague 1978: Vainio's Mad Sprint

Two Romanians led for most of the race, with Ilie Floroiu passing halfway in a swift 13:44.8, close to world-record pace. Two kilometers later, a staggering dozen runners remained in contention. Observers had trouble believing their stopwatches.

A few laps farther on, eight remained in the hunt. Martti Vainio of Finland, a "relative unknown" before the race, struggled at the back of the pack. At 9K, Britain's Dave Black took over. He lasted until the final 300, when the terrific pace broke him. Brendan Foster, the world record-holder until 10 weeks earlier at 27:30.3, led until the final turn.

That's when Vainio and two other "unknowns," Venanzio Ortis of Italy and Aleksandr Antipov of the Soviet Union, attacked. Vainio grabbed the lead and struggled to hold it as the other two crept closer on the last stretch. The Finn hit the line in 27:31.0, as the next two both clocked 27:31.5. Seven of the top 10 broke their national records in what many considered to be the greatest 10,000-meter race ever.

## FINAL RESULTS (8/29)
1. Martti Vainio (Finland) ...........................21:31.0
2. Venanzio Ortis (Italy) ............................27:31.5
3. Aleksandr Antipov (Soviet Union) ...........27:31.5
4. Brendan Foster (Great Britain) ................27:32.7
5. Dave Black (Great Britain) .......................27:36.3
6. Gerard Tebroke (Netherlands)..................27:36.6
7. Ilie Floroiu (Romania)..............................27:40.1
8. Enn Sellik (Soviet Union) .........................27:40.6

# No. 33 -- World Championships Women's 10,000, Seville 1999: Wami vs. Radcliffe

Paula Radcliffe knew she couldn't kick, and she knew that meant her chances for gold were severely limited by the presence of Ethiopian Gete Wami, a fierce finisher. She also knew that to even have a chance for a medal, she would have to run the race of her life.

That she did. The 25-year-old Briton started out hard and kept upping the ante. She hit 5K in 15:25.25, and only three others were still with her. A few laps later, marathon world record-holder Tegla Loroupe shot into the lead and Olympic champion Fernanda Ribeiro dropped out. Then Radcliffe went to the fore again, hoping to burn off Wami.

The Ethiopian never blinked. With 300 meters left, she exploded into the lead, winning in 30:24.56. Radcliffe clocked 30:27.13, as the three medalists all broke their national records. Radcliffe, as realistic as she is tough, showed no bitterness at leading only to be outkicked. After all, she had authored the greatest women's 10,000-meter run ever.

## FINAL RESULTS (8/26)
1. Geta Wami (Ethiopia)............................ 30:24.56
2. Paula Radcliffe (Great Britain).............. 30:27.13
3. Tegla Loroupe (Kenya) ........................... 30:32.03
4. Harumi Hiroyama (Japan) ..................... 31:26.84
5. Chiemi Takahashi (Japan) ..................... 31:27.62
6. Merima Hashim (Ethiopia)..................... 31:32.06
7. Berhane Adere (Ethiopia) ....................... 31:32.51
8. Teresa Recio (Spain) .............................. 31:43.80

# No. 32 -- World Cup Men's 800, Düsseldorf 1977: Juantorena vs. Boit

Great expectations awaited the showdown between Olympic champion Alberto Juantorena of Cuba and Mike Boit, the Kenyan favorite who had been kept from the Montreal Olympics by the African boycott. Their first encounter, at Zurich a week earlier, had featured a brutally fast pace that saw Juantorena win in 1:43.64 to Boit's 1:44.64.

In Düsseldorf, the pace was more sane, with India's Sri Ram Singh leading at 400 in 52.31. The Cuban ran second, with Boit a step back in third. On the backstretch, the two passed the Indian. Juantorena hit 600 in 1:18.9, and Boit attacked. He barely made a dent with his furious charge, as Juantorena held him off. On the straight, Juantorena looked for Boit. He didn't have to look far.

Boit pulled even and the two ran side-by-side to the finish, both sprinting desperately. A few steps from the line, Juantorena edged ahead, claiming the win in 1:44.04 to Boit's 1:44.14. Boit, who had run his last 200 in 25.0, maintained that he had started his kick too soon. His rival said he was never worried.

Said Juantorena, "It was really a tough race. Mike Boit was as tough as I expected."

## FINAL RESULTS (9/2)

1. Alberto Juantorena (Cuba) .................. 1:44.04
2. Mike Boit (Kenya)................................. 1:44.14
3. Willi Wülbeck (West Germany)............. 1:45.47
4. Mark Enyeart (USA)............................ 1:45.52
5. Jozef Plachy (Czechoslovakia)............... 1:45.53
6. John Higham (Australia)....................... 1:46.15
7. Olaf Beyer (East Germany)................... 1:46.59
8. Sri Ram Singh (India).......................... 1:47.28

# No. 31 -- Olympic Men's 100, Helsinki 1952: Remigino vs. McKenley

Lindy Remigino [*Manhattan College*]

Lindy Remigino had no business being in the Olympic final. He had only placed third in the IC4A 100 that spring, and fifth in the NCAA. At the AAU Championships, the Manhattan College junior couldn't even make the final. But when Jim Golliday got injured before the Trials, and Andy Stanfield decided to concentrate on the 200, Remigino had a chance.

At the Trials, he placed a surprising second to Art Bragg. Then Bragg turned up injured at the Games. In the final, Remigino was shocked by being one of the leaders in a blanket finish. The top four finished within a few feet of each other. He congratulated Jamaican Herb McKenley, whom he thought had won. Then came the reading of the finish photo, followed by Remigino's immortal quote to McKenley, "Gosh, Herb. It looks as though I won the darn thing."

In 1999, Remigino wrote to me after I first published an account of this race: "In the final I led from start to finish, and leaned too soon, barely winning in 10.4. Herb McKenley did pass me after the finish, and my remarks were as you quoted. Herb, Harrison Dillard and Art Bragg and I have remained close friends."

## FINAL RESULTS (7/29)
1. Lindy Remigino (USA).............................10.4    (10.79)
2. Herb McKenley (Jamaica) ........................10.4    (10.80)
3. McDonald Bailey (Great Britain)..............10.4    (10.83)
4. Dean Smith (USA)...................................10.4    (10.84)
5. Vladimir Sukharev (Soviet Union)............10.5    (10.88)
6. John Treloar (Australia)...........................10.5    (10.91)

# No. 30 -- Olympic Men's Hammer, Melbourne 1956: Connolly over Krivonosov

Hal Connolly played a part in two of the greatest dramas of the Games, but most remember him just for one. He fell in love with Czech thrower Olga Connolly in Melbourne, and their Iron Curtain romance intrigued many in the year it took to get the Communist government in Czechoslovakia to agree to their marriage.

On the field, Connolly posed other problems for the Reds. Mikhail Krivonosov of the Soviet Union held the world record in the hammer. Connolly opened up with a long heave that went foul. Krivonosov then took the lead in round two with a throw of 206 feet, 8 inches (63.00). Connolly crept close in round three with a 205-6 (62.65), but Krivonosov added an inch (206-9/63.03). Then in round five, Connolly hurled an Olympic record 207-3 (63.19). The Russian could not respond.

Connolly continued to improve over the next few years, and by 1965, owned seven of history's eight longest throws. However, while he still owns the gold, his marriage to Olga lasted only 17 years. Connolly's son (by a second marriage), Adam, threw 237-5 (72.37) in 1999, placing 4th that year in both the NCAA and the USA Championships.

## FINAL RESULTS (11/24)
1. Hal Connolly (USA) .................................. 63.19     207-3
2. Mikhail Krivonosov (Soviet Union) ......... 63.03     206-9
3. Anatoli Samotsvetov (Soviet Union) ....... 62.56     205-3
4. Al Hall (USA).......................................... 61.96     203-3
5. Jozsef Csermak (Hungary)...................... 60.70     199-2
6. Krešimir Račić (Yugoslavia)................... 60.36     198-0
7. Dmitriy Egorov (Soviet Union)............... 60.22     197-7
8. Sverre Strandli (Norway)....................... 59.21     194-3

# No. 29 -- Olympic Trials Men's 400 Hurdles, Indianapolis 1988: Moses vs. Phillips

A year earlier, three men had broken 48 seconds in the World Championships; it was the first time that so many had run so fast over the one-lap hurdles. The field in Indianapolis topped that.

The legendary Edwin Moses reigned supreme, leading the field from the start. Kevin Young ran close behind, but hit the ninth hurdle. That left Andre Phillips as Moses' closest challenger, with Danny Harris, the man who had ended the King's winning streak, closing fast.

As Young recovered and caught Harris, David Patrick produced a blistering finish out of lane one. While Moses (47.37) and Phillips (47.58) finished 1-2, Young (47.72), Patrick (47.75) and Harris (47.76) crossed together. It was the fastest mass finish ever, yet only the top three qualified for the Olympics, leaving two of the fastest six runners in history home to watch it on TV.

Said Moses, "I felt really good. I was in control. I ran my own race and that's the key to winning."

## FINAL RESULTS (7/17)
1. Edwin Moses (adidas) ........................................ 47.37
2. Andre Phillips (West Coast AC) ......................... 47.58
3. Kevin Young (Santa Monica TC) ...................... 47.72
4. David Patrick (Stars & Stripes TC) .................. 47.75
5. Danny Harris (Athletics West) ......................... 47.76
6. Tranel Hawkins (Accusplit) ............................. 48.65
7. Kevin Henderson (Atlantic Coast Club)............ 49.28
8. Pat McGhee (Iowa) .......................................... 49.32

# No. 28 -- World Championships Women's 100, Stuttgart 1993: Devers vs. Ottey

As much as this race mirrored other fantastically close dash finishes we have seen from the top women over the past decade, it also highlighted the great differences in the attitudes of the winners versus the losers.

Four women figured to be in the mix: Gwen Torrence, Russia's Irina Privalova, Jamaican Merlene Ottey, and Gail Devers, attempting a dash/hurdles double. Privalova led for much of the first half of the race before succumbing to the speed of Devers.

Ottey then pulled even with the compact American in the final meters, and appeared to have a slight lead with a step to go. Then Devers threw her body into a lean at the finish, while the tall Jamaican remained relatively upright.

Replays of the stadium video didn't help the crowd separate the two. Finally, the announcer hailed Devers as the winner, 10.81 to 10.82. The Jamaicans immediately protested. Said Devers, "The protest doesn't bother me at all. I need to focus on the hurdles now. This race is over."

Ottey told the press, "If the protest goes against me, it will be the wrong decision." After a couple hours, the panel, not unanimously, declared Devers victorious, with a corrected time of 10.82. The photo showed a margin of just 0.004 seconds, or one centimeter. Ottey lashed out, "I'm the champion. They made a mistake but won't admit it."

## FINAL RESULTS (8/16)
1. Gail Devers (USA) .................... 10.82
2. Merlene Ottey (Jamaica) .......... 10.82
3. Gwen Torrence (USA) .............. 10.89
4. Irina Privalova (Russia) ........... 10.96
5. Mary Onyali (Nigeria).............. 11.05
6. Natalya Voronova (Russia) ....... 11.20
7. Nikole Mitchell (Jamaica)......... 11.20
8. Liliana Allen (Cuba) ................. 11.23

# No. 27 -- Olympic Men's 5,000, Montreal 1976: Viren over Quax

This is the race that legions of Steve Prefontaine worshippers are in denial about; had the American star not been killed in a 1975 car crash, they insist, he would have won gold in Montreal.

Fat chance. Four years earlier, Finland's Lasse Viren destroyed Pre and the rest of the 5,000-meter field with a 4:01.2 final mile. Here, he set out to win his fourth gold medal. Never before had anyone won the Olympic 5,000 twice. And the deck seemed stacked against Viren. He had already raced 25,000 meters in the previous week, running the heats and final of the 10K, plus a 5,000 heat.

His competition included several faster men who could be trouble in a slow race, especially if Viren showed signs of fatigue. New Zealanders Dick Quax and Rod Dixon both had better speed credentials. After seven laps at a solid pace, Viren took the lead, to slow the race down. He was tired. Over the next few laps, the lead changed hands several times.

With a kilometer to go, Viren took over again. Brendan Foster passed him, but the Finn quickly regained the lead. At the bell lap, the top five were separated by 0.4 seconds. With 300 left, Ian Stewart made his bid, but Viren fought him off. Dixon made a powerful move on the last turn, but Viren easily lengthened his stride and pulled away. Then, on the straightaway, Quax sprinted to pull even with the Finn, but like all the others, he could not beat him.

Viren won in 13:24.76. Exhausted? Sure, but a few days later he also placed fifth in the marathon.

## FINAL RESULTS (7/30)
1. Lasse Virén (Finland) .................................... 13:24.76
2. Dick Quax (New Zealand) ............................. 13:25.16
3. Klaus-Peter Hildenbrand (West Germany).... 13:25.38
4. Rod Dixon (New Zealand) ............................. 13:25.50
5. Brendan Foster (Great Britain) ..................... 13:26.19
6. Willy Polleunis (Belgium) ............................. 13:26.99
7. Ian Stewart (Great Britain) .......................... 13:27.65
8. Aniceto Simões (Portugal) ............................ 13:29.38

# No. 26 — Olympic Trials Women's 100 Hurdles, Los Angeles 1984: Turner vs. Fitzgerald

If a great race is defined as a close one, the Trials 100 hurdles took the cake. Stephanie Hightower and Kim Turner (later McKenzie) led early, with Benita Fitzgerald joining the party at midway. Then Pam Page closed fast in the final stages.

All four cleared the final hurdle evenly, and when they dipped at the finish, silence reigned. The human eye could not tell who the top three were, let alone who won. The finish was shown repeatedly on the stadium screen, but it did little to settle matters.

The head of the photo-finish panel said that it was the closest race he had ever seen, but the results were clear: Turner won in 13.12, with Fitzgerald (13.13) in second, Page (13.13) in third, and Hightower (13.13) in fourth. The margin from first to fourth was less than the width of this page.

## FINAL RESULTS (6/23)
1. Kim Turner (Bud Lite TC) .................. 13.12
2. Benita Fitzgerald (adidas) .................. 13.13
3. Pam Page (Puma Energizer).............. 13.13
4. Stephanie Hightower (Bud Lite)......... 13.13
5. Candy Young (Puma Energizer) ......... 13.26
6. Pat Davis (St. Augustine) .................. 13.40
7. Linda Weekly (Atoms) ....................... 13.54
8. Arnita Epps (Texas Southern) ............ 13.80

# No. 25 -- Olympic Decathlon, Rome 1960: Johnson vs. Yang

C.K. Yang [*Associated Students, University of California, Los Angeles*]

Rafer Johnson and C.K. Yang were friends and UCLA teammates. The Olympic decathlon, however, put them in different uniforms. Johnson, an American, was favored over the man who was known in Taiwan as Yang Chuan-kwang.

On day one, both performed as expected, Johnson finishing the long day (it ended after midnight) with a 55-point lead. At the start of day two, the American hit disaster in the hurdles. With a PR of 13.8, he could manage only 15.3, handing Yang a 128-point lead. Johnson popped a great discus throw, getting 144 points ahead. In the vault, Yang pulled to within 24 points.

Johnson started the final event, 1,500 meters, 67 points ahead of his friend. He knew he would have to stay in contact with Yang, who needed a nine-second margin to take the gold. Johnson did it, finishing 1.2 seconds behind. His gold medal score of 8,392 translates to 7,901 on the current scoring tables. It was his final decathlon.

## FINAL RESULTS (9/6)

1. Rafer Johnson (USA) ............................. 8392
*(10.9, 7.35/24-1½, 15.82/51-11, 1.85/6-¾, 48.3, 15.3, 48.49, 4.10/13-5¼, 69.76/228-10, 4:49.7)*
2. C.K. Yang (China-Taiwan) ...................... 8334
*(10.7, 7.46/24-5¾, 13.33/43-8¾, 1.90/6-2¾, 48.1, 14.6, 39.83, 4.30/14-1¼, 68.22/223-10, 4:48.5)*
3. Vasili Kuznetsov (Soviet Union) ............ 7809
4. Yuri Kutenko (Soviet Union) ................. 7567
5. Everet Kamerbeek (Netherlands) ........... 7236
6. Franco Sar (Italy) ................................. 7195
7. Markus Kahma (Finland) ...................... 7112
8. Klaus Grogorenz (Germany) ................. 7032

# No. 24 -- AAU Men's 400, Philadelphia 1941: Klemmer Ties Record

Grover Klemmer [*University of California - Berkeley*]

While much of the rest of the world was enmeshed in World War II, America waited in 1941 for the other shoe to drop. Long before many of them had heard of Pearl Harbor, the American athletes still trained. The year before, their Olympics had been cancelled; what they future held, they could not guess.

Yet there were great runners competing, and one was Cal's Grover Klemmer. He had set a world record in the 440 by clocking 46.4 to win the Pacific Coast Conference (forerunner of the Pac-10). That mark was inferior to the 400-meter best of 46.0, held by Germany's Rudolf Harbig.

At Philadelphia's Franklin Field, Klemmer lined up with his rivals from USC, Hubie Kerns and Cliff Bourland, to settle the national championship. All were tired, having run their heats less than an hour before. The runners went out fast, hitting 200 in 21.8 on the one-turn course.

Klemmer led the tiring sprinters home, but he was not alone. It would be one of the closest, and fastest, one-lap races of all time. Klemmer clocked 46.0 to tie the world record. At 46.1, both Kerns and Bourland crossed, and Al Diebolt ran a great 46.4 in fourth.

## FINAL RESULTS (6/29)

1. Grover Klemmer .................. 46.0    world record
2. Hubert Kerns ........................ 46.1
3. Cliff Bourland ...................... 46.1
4. Alfred Diebolt ...................... 46.4
5. James Herbert ...................... 46.8
6. John Campbell ...................... 46.9
Harold Bogrow ......................... dnf

# No. 23 -- Olympic Trials Men's 200 - South Lake Tahoe 1968: Carlos vs. Smith

John Carlos and Tommie Smith trained together and raced together, and the two stood atop the world. At the final Olympic Trials, when they lined up for their 200 showdown, silence ruled. Until Larry Questad "let out a yelp" when he saw an ant near his hand.

A few minutes later, ant relocated, the race started. Carlos ran the best turn and led Questad and Jerry Bright by two yards as they entered the straightaway. Smith, running in lane one, lagged behind until the final 40 meters. He exploded toward the finish, but he could not overtake Carlos, who hit the line in a world-record 19.7. Smith grabbed second in 20.0, with Questad third in 20.1. Their electronic times were 19.92, 20.18, and 20.28.

Carlos' performance would be denied official recognition because he (as well as Smith) had worn 68-pin brush spikes, illegal under IAAF rules. A few months later at the Olympics, Smith would upend his friend in another great race, but his accomplishment would be overshadowed by the protest the two would make on the victory stand in Mexico City.

## FINAL RESULTS (6/30)

1. John Carlos (Santa Clara Valley YV) .......... 19.7    (19.92) world record
2. Tommie Smith (Santa Clara Valley YV) ...... 20.0    (20.18)
3. Larry Questad (Striders) ............................ 20.1    (20.28)
4. Jerry Bright (Arizona State) ........................ 20.1    (20.29)
5. Tom Randolph (Western Michigan) ............. 20.1    (20.29)
6. Bill Bruckel (U.S. Navy) ............................. 20.3    (20.52)

# No. 22 -- Olympic 5,000, Paris 1924: Nurmi vs. Ritola

This is really the story of four races, and goes a long way to explaining why the term "immortal" so automatically connects itself to the name of Finland's Paavo Nurmi.

The stoic Finn wanted to win both the 1,500 and 5,000 in the Paris Games, a feat considered impossible since the events took place within one hour. In Helsinki, three weeks prior to the Games, he tried to simulate the double. His results of 3:52.6 and 14:28.2 ·· both world records ·· stunned observers.

In Paris, he won the 1,500 by burning off his rivals with a four-minute mile pace for the first half, then gliding in to a 3:53.6. Forty-two minutes later, he lined up for the 5,000. His opponents knew what they had to do, and went out hard, well under record pace. Nurmi stayed close. At the halfway mark, he took over, and only his teammate Ville Ritola could keep up. Nurmi crossed the line in 14:31.2, the second-fastest time in history. No one has succeeded in winning that double since.

The Flying Finn wasn't done, however. Two days later, he won the 10K cross country race by 400 meters on a day so hot that 23 of the 38 runners could not finish. The next day, he led Finland to victory in the 3K team race, just missing the world record with an 8:32.0.

## FINAL RESULTS (7/10)
1. Paavo Nurmi (Finland) ......................... 14:31.2
2. Ville Ritola (Finland) ........................... 14:31.4
3. Edvin Wide (Sweden) ........................... 15:01.8
4. John Romig (USA) ................................ 15:12.4
5. Eino Seppälä (Finland) ........................ 15:18.4
6. Charles Clibbon (Great Britain)............ 15:29.0
7. Lucien Dolques (France) ...................... 15:32.6
8. Axel Eriksson (Sweden) ....................... 15:38.0

# No. 21 -- Golden Gala Men's Pole Vault, Rome 1984: Bubka vs. Vigneron

Thierry Vigneron had just won the Olympic bronze and was the hottest vaulter on the circuit. World champion Sergei Bubka held the world record at 19-4.25, but had been boycotted out of the Games. Their match-up in Rome was eagerly anticipated.

A year earlier, Vigneron had leapt a record 19-1.5. This time, when both men cleared 19-2, Bubka led, clearing by a huge amount. Call it pressure. "I must win," Vigneron had told the press. He missed his first try at a new record, 19-4.75. Bubka was called on a time foul. Then, on Vigneron's second attempt, he cleared.

While the Frenchman celebrated, Bubka passed. The bar went up to 19-5.75. Vigneron signaled that he would pass. Just minutes after he lost his world record, Bubka hefted himself well over the bar, faintly brushing it on his way down. It was the only time in history the world record was raised twice in a single competition.

Vigneron took his last jumps at 19-7, Bubka at 19-8.25. Both failed. Yet this marked a day that 1980 Olympic champ Wladislaw Kozakiewicz had heralded a few months earlier: "I think the reign of Bubka has just begun." Vigneron's 10-minute hold on the record would be the last time another man held it. Over the course of his career, Bubka would raise the outdoor world record 17 times and the indoor record 18.

## FINAL RESULTS (8/31)

1. Sergey Bubka (Soviet Union)..................5.94    19-5¾  world record
2. Thierry Vigneron (France)......................5.91    19-4¾
3. Aleksandr Krupskiy (Soviet Union)........5.70    18-8¼
4. Joe Dial (USA)........................................5.60    18-4½
=5. Marian Kolasa (Poland........................5.60    18-4½
=5. Earl Bell (USA)....................................5.60    18-4½
7. Patrick Abada (France)..........................5.50    18-½
8. Atanas Tarev (Bulgaria).........................5.40    17-8½

# No. 20 -- Olympic Men's 5,000, Helsinki 1952: Zátopek Rules

Four years earlier, Czechoslovakia's Emil Zátopek was largely an unknown when he won the 10,000 and missed gold in the 5,000 by mere inches. In Helsinki, however, he was both known and feared. All knew of his crazy experiments with interval training, with running in heavy boots. They might even have laughed at his horrid form if he had been slower.

In Helsinki, Zátopek wanted to win the double that eluded him in London. He had no problem with the 10,000, winning by 100 yards in an Olympic record. In the 5,000, however, the field would not be so easy to dominate. Zátopek counted among his rivals Alain Mimoun, Gordon Pirie, defending champion Gaston Reiff and Herbert Schade, who was also a friend.

Before the race, Zátopek advised Schade to avoid the lead for the first 2K. The crowd of 66,000 made plenty of noise, however, and the nervous Schade passed Chris Chataway at 800 meters. Twice Zátopek tried to pass Schade in order to take the burden of leading off him. Twice Schade fought back for the lead. Finally, the Czech yelled at him, "Do two laps with me, Herbert!"

Zátopek led for a while, before Schade moved ahead again. Then Pirie took over. With two laps left, six men were in the hunt. With the tension of 500 meters left, Reiff dropped out. Then the pack swept past Pirie. At the bell, Zátopek made his move to the front. Instead of crumbling, his three pursuers stayed on him. Coming off the next turn, Chataway blasted past, then Schade and Mimoun.

But Chataway had sprinted too soon, and on the final straightaway, both Schade and Mimoun pulled even. Then from Zátopek came a burst of amazing speed. He caught them. The four sprinted side by side, but at the end, it was all Zátopek, the "Human Locomotive." He won in 14:06.6. He wasn't done. On the last day of the Games, he entered his first marathon. He won his third gold of the week by a half-mile.

## FINAL RESULTS (7/24)

1. Emil Zátopek (Czechoslovakia) ............. 14:06.6
2. Alain Mimoun (France) ........................ 14:07.4
3. Herbert Schade (Germany) ................... 14:08.6
4. Gordon Pirie (Great Britain) ................ 14:18.0
5. Chris Chataway (Great Britain) ........... 14:18.0
6. Les Perry (Australia) ............................ 14:23.6
7. Ernõ Béres (Hungary) ......................... 14:24.8
8. Åke Andersson (Sweden) ...................... 14:26.0

# No. 19 -- World Championships Men's 4 x 400 Relay, Tokyo 1991: Britain vs. the United States

Many Americans have felt that the 4 x 4 gold somehow belongs to the United States, no matter who wins it. Great Britain, despite not having won an Olympic or World gold in the event since 1936, did not subscribe to that thinking.

While the British lined up a surprisingly strong team -- leading off with 400 silver medalist Roger Black -- the Americans bickered over the make-up of their team. The U.S. foursome had been selected from the top finishers in the 400 at the nationals. Michael Johnson, the No. 1-ranked quarter miler, had only run the 200 there. Said Quincy Watts, "If Michael Johnson wanted to be on this team, he should have run the 400."

When Gabriel Luke came up injured, coach Tom Tellez offered Johnson a spot in the 4 x 400 heats. He declined. The Brits produced a 2:59.49 in the heats, faster than the Americans. In the final, "the idea was to break America's heart early," quipped British coach Frank Dick. Black led off in 44.7. Andrew Valmon ran a step behind.

On the second leg, Derek Redmond blasted a 44.0, but was still run down by the 43.4 of Quincy Watts. Danny Everett ran the third leg for the U.S. in 44.31, but John Regis narrowed the gap with his 44.22. It came down to a duel between 400 champion Antonio Pettigrew and Kriss Akabusi, who had won bronze in the 400H.

On the first turn, a TV crew got in the way, causing Pettigrew to shout and miss a step. Akabusi stayed on him until the final stretch, when he attacked. The two fought their way to the finish, the Briton edging ahead only in the final strides, 2:57.53 to 2:57.57. "It was a great race," said Pettigrew, "but we will be back."

## FINAL RESULTS (9/1)

1. Great Britain ................................ 2:57.53
*(Roger Black 44.7, Derek Redmond 44.0, John Regis 44.22, Kriss Akabusi 44.59)*
2. United States ............................... 2:57.57
*(Andrew Valmon 44.9, Quincy Watts 43.4, D. Everett 44.31, A. Pettigrew 44.93)*
3. Jamaica ...................................... 3:00.10
4. Yugoslavia .................................. 3:00.32
5. Kenya ......................................... 3:00.34
6. Germany ..................................... 3:00.75
7. Morocco ...................................... 3:04.49
8. Cuba ........................................... 3:05.33

# No. 18 — Olympic Trials Men's 800, Los Angeles 1984: Jones vs. Gray

The American record of 1:43.91 by Rick Wohlhuter had stood for 10 years. In that time, U.S. two-lapping had stagnated, with few challenging the top man, seven-time U.S. champ James Robinson. Earl Jones changed all that.

The sophomore from Eastern Michigan hadn't even qualified for the NCAA 800 the previous year. But a 1:44.5 relay leg in the spring of 1984 had him thinking of bigger things. In the Trials final, he went out hard, leading through 200 in 24.2. At 400, he passed the line in 50.2, with only Stanley Redwine running close. John Marshall and Johnny Gray held back.

At 600, Jones led in 1:16.7. Robinson, in seventh, began making his move. Ahead of him, Gray and Marshall caught Redwine. The expected demise of Jones never happened. Gray came the closest to beating him, missing by an inch, with Marshall a step behind. Robinson ran the race of his life, and finished nearly even with Marshall. He would have to wait until the final results to see if he had made the team.

Both Jones and Gray had run an American record 1:43.74. Marshall got third in 1:43.92, and Robinson, in heart-breaking fourth, clocked the same 1:43.92. It was the fastest time of his life, just a hundredth away from the record he had been chasing for years, and it didn't even get him on the team.

Jones earned bronze in the Games later that summer, and for two years remained one of the world's best half-milers. A car accident then left him with a severely damaged leg, ending his career at age 22.

## FINAL RESULTS (6/19)
1. Earl Jones (Eastern Michigan) .......... 1:43.74  American record
2. Johnny Gray (Santa Monica TC) ....... 1:43.74  American record
3. John Marshall (Villanova) ................. 1:43.92
4. James Robinson (Inter City AC) ........ 1:43.92
5. Don Paige (Athletes Attic) ................. 1:45.17
6. Stanley Redwine (Athletics West) ...... 1:45.32
7. Pete Richardson (Arizona State) ........ 1:46.64
8. Eugene Sanders (Bud Lite) ............... 1:47.05

# No. 17 -- Olympic Men's Discus, Montreal 1976: Wilkins over Powell

The viewers at home were looking for an American hero, up close and personal. If they didn't already know Mac Wilkins, they didn't know what to make of him. He looked like a wildman with his long hair and beard. He openly criticized the U.S. Olympic Committee, stirring the storm even further by saying he hoped East Germany would win all the medals. The USOC president called him a "grandstander and a pop-off."

Then, rather than being friends with America's other top thrower, John Powell, Wilkins didn't even fake it. His best friend in the competition was the man who was supposed to be the enemy, East German Wolfgang Schmidt.

Wilkins, calm despite the controversy, knew what he had to do to crush Powell psychologically. In the qualifying round, on his first throw in the still air of the partially enclosed stadium, he produced a crushing heave of 224-0 (68.28). Powell conceded: "I don't see how he can be stopped."

The next day, Wilkins threw 221-5 (67.50) in round two. Powell managed a 215-7 (65.70) in response. Schmidt, who had been in fourth, moved to third with a 213-9 (65.16). In the fourth round, many thought he had produced a throw better than Powell's, but an official called him on a toe violation. Schmidt's argument went nowhere. Wilkins consoled him.

In the last round, Schmidt came through, launching the platter out to 217-3 (66.22) to take the silver from Powell. Wilkins and he celebrated with a bear hug as Powell stalked off. Later, Powell said, "You're a fool if you don't think that winning is everything."

## FINAL RESULTS (7/25)

1. Mac Wilkins (USA) ..................................... 67.50      221-5
*(61.78/202-8, 67.50/221-5, 63.44/208-2, 63.52/208-5, foul, 66.14/217-0)*
2. Wolfgang Schmidt (East Germany) ............ 66.22      217-3
*(63.68/208-11, foul, 65.16/213-9, foul, 63.96/209-10, 66.22/217-3)*
3. John Powell (USA) ..................................... 65.70      215-7
*(62.48/205-0, 64.24/210-9, 65.70/215-7, 60.48/198-5, 60.20/197-6, 64.24/210-9)*
4. Norbert Thiede (East Germany) .................. 64.30      210-11
5. Siegfried Pachale (East Germany) .............. 64.24      210-9
6. Pentti Kahma (Finland) ............................. 63.12      207-1
7. Knut Hjeltnes (Norway) ............................ 63.06      206-11
8. Jay Silvester (USA) ................................... 61.98      203-4

# No. 16 -- Olympic Men's 200, Mexico City 1968: Smith vs. Carlos

Most of what fans remember about this race is the still-controversial awards ceremony protest. Love them or hate them, you have to concede that the men who made the protest also made one of the greatest furlong races ever.

Both John Carlos and Tommie Smith were capable of world records. Their closest rival, Australian Peter Norman, wasn't far off, bringing his best down to 20.2 at high altitude in the weeks leading up to the Games.

With the help of Mexico City's thin air, the Olympic record was tied or broken five times before the top eight even stepped on the track for the final. After the second semifinal race, Tommie Smith limped off with a cramp. The finals were only two hours away. "I didn't think I was going to make it," he said.

In the final, Carlos ran a lightning turn, and had a solid lead at the top of the straightaway. Smith, his cramp vanished, drove hard and caught his friend with 60 meters left. Norman, only sixth after the turn, finished fast. As Smith approached the line, he threw both his hands up in jubilation, crossing in a world record 19.83. A tiring Carlos looked to his left to watch Smith finish, oblivious to Norman coming hard on his right. Norman snatched the silver away in the final steps, 20.06 to 20.10.

## FINAL RESULTS (10/16)
1. Tommie Smith (USA)...............................19.83  world record
2. Peter Norman (Australia) .........................20.06
3. John Carlos (USA) ....................................20.10
4. Edwin Roberts (Trinidad) .........................20.34
5. Roger Bambuck (France) ..........................20.51
6. Larry Questad (USA)...............................20.62
7. Michael Fray (Jamaica) ...........................20.63
8. Joachim Eigenherr (West Germany).........20.66

# No. 15 — Penn Relays Men's Distance Medley, Philadelphia 1987: Georgetown vs. Arkansas

Many fans feel that it doesn't get any better than relay races for excitement. And no meet has hosted more great stick races than the Penn Relays. Director Dave Johnson points out that the 4-x-mile used to be the meet finale, and a thrilling 1912 race on a muddy track saw Cambridge beat Penn by three yards.

Though few could compare the races, the 1987 distance medley may have been even better. Arkansas held the world best of 9:22.6 from the previous year, and had a tougher foursome this time around. Still, the Hogs were only in fourth at the first hand-off, as Mount St. Mary's Charles Cheruiyot led in 2:50.9 for the 1200 leg. Then Arkansas' Roddie Haley got the stick. The autotimer caught him in 44.41 for the blazing lap in which he ran down Indiana, Villanova, and Mount St. Mary's. Lorenzo Brown took over for the 800 leg, covering two laps in 1:46.9. Miles Irish of Georgetown chased him, and brought the Hoyas into the hunt with his 1:46.1.

Arkansas' Doug Consiglio started the 1,600 anchor leg with an eight-meter lead, but the Mount's Kip Cheruiyot sprinted to catch him on the first lap. Also joining the party were Gerry O'Reilly of Villanova and Georgetown's Mike Stahr. For two laps they stayed together, then Consiglio fell off the back.

On the final lap, Stahr pushed hard, but couldn't lose O'Reilly. The two strained to the finish line, with Stahr prevailing in 3:54.9 to O'Reilly's 3:55.3. Georgetown, with its All-America squad, won in 9:20.96, as the first three teams all broke the world best. Said Stahr, "I just focused on the finish line."

## FINAL RESULTS (4/25)

1. Georgetown..........................9:20.96   world record
*(John Trautmann 2:53.1, Darron Outler 46.9, Miles Irish 1:46.1, Mike Stahr 3:54.9)*
2. Villanova ...........................9:21.02
*(Sean O'Neill 2:52.0, E. Modibedi 45.3, Bruce Harris 1:48.5, Gerry O'Reilly 3:55.3)*
3. Mount St. Mary's................9:21.66
*(Charles Cheruiyot 2:50.9, D. Lishebo 45.8, P. Rono 1:47.9, Kip Cheruiyot 3:57.1)*
4. Arkansas ............................9:25.56
*(Gary Taylor 2:52.1, Roddie Haley 44.41, L. Brown 1:46.9, Doug Consiglio 4:02.2)*
5. Indiana ..............................9:27.65
6. Navy ..................................9:31.25
7. Penn State.........................9:31.62
8. Manhattan..........................9:33.40

# No. 14 — Olympic Trials Women's 1,500, Los Angeles 1984: Wysocki vs. Decker

When Ruth Wysocki made the Olympic team in the 800 with a PR 1:59.34, that was a dream-come-true comeback for the former age group star. The 1,500 final, five days later, she ran with hopes of getting a personal record and maybe another team slot.

That's because Mary Decker ruled. The previous summer, she had won world titles in the 1,500 and 3,000. She hadn't been beaten by another American on the track in four years. She had already clocked a 3:59.19 in 1984, and so no one predicted a 4:13 runner like Wysocki would give her a problem.

Decker led from the start, but her pace was modest enough (2:11.5 at 800) that with 300 meters left, six rivals still followed closely. The one who struck first was Wysocki, who later said, "I expected Decker to blast off." Around the turn the two battled, with Decker gaining a slight lead by the time they reached the homestretch. Then Wysocki inexorably pounded ahead. She won by a stride in 4:00.18, becoming the second-fastest American ever, with Decker crossing a step later in 4:00.40.

Wysocki later told *Track and Field News*, "My reaction was, 'What have I done?' "

## FINAL RESULTS (6/24)
1. Ruth Wysocki (Brooks)..............................4:00.18
2. Mary Decker (Athletics West)...................4:00.40
3. Diana Richburg (Gazelle International)....4:04.07
4. Missy Kane (adidas)................................4:06.47
5. Sue Addison (Athletics West)....................4:06.91
6. Darlene Beckford (Liberty AC) ................4:07.42
7. Louise Romo (California) ........................4:09.29
8. Chris Gregorek (Athletics West)..............4:09.43

# No. 13 -- Olympic Decathlon, Los Angeles 1984: Thompson vs. Hingsen

In the years leading up to their Olympic confrontation, Daley Thompson had beaten Jurgen Hingsen four times straight, three of those being world records. That didn't mean that beating the German was easy, for Thompson or anybody else. Hingsen came prepared, but Thompson came hot. He got his best start ever, with a 10.44 dash, a 26-3½ (8.01) decathlon record in the long jump, and a personal-record shot. It wasn't until the high jump that Hingsen (6-11½/2.12) started narrowing the points gap. In the 400, both went nuts, but Thompson went a lot more nuts. His 46.97 (to Hingsen's 47.69) gave him the best-ever first day, 4,633 points.

On day two, the discus proved critical. Hingsen threw 166-9 (50.82), the best ever in the Olympics. Thompson was at only 135-4 (41.24) after two throws. On his third, he went wild and whipped it out to 152-9 (46.56), another personal record. Thompson led by 32 points.

With three events left, Hingsen had every chance to win. The pole vault, however, proved to be his downfall. A 16-foot (4.88) performer, he barely cleared 14-9 (4.50) and could go no higher. A sudden illness had him vomiting. Thompson, meanwhile, vaulted 16-4¾ (5.00). It was all over, except for Thompson's world-record chase, which was looking like a sure bet. Thompson nailed the javelin, and in the 1,500, had only to run 4:34.8 to break Hingsen's record. No problem for him usually, but he came up dry. He ran 4:35.0 and missed by a point. "There are other times to break the record," he said.

Quipped Hingsen, "Someday I'll beat him. Of course, I may be 80 by then." Ironically, new decathlon scoring tables were adopted the next season, and Thompson's performance was retroactively ratified as the world record at 8,847 points, under the new math 15 points better than Hingsen's old standard.

## FINAL RESULTS (8/8-9)

1. Daley Thompson (Great Britain) ..............8797    (8847) world record
*(10.44, 8.01/26-3½, 15.72/51-7, 2.03/6-8, 46.97, 14.33, 46.56/152-9, 5.00/16-4¾, 65.24/214-0, 4:35.00)*
2. Jürgen Hingsen (West Germany) .............8673    (8695)
3. Siggi Wentz (West Germany)...................8412    (8416)
4. Guido Kratschmer (West Germany) .........8326    (8357)
5. Billy Motti (France) ................................8266    (8278)
6. John Crist (USA) ....................................8130    (8115)
7. Jim Wooding (USA) ................................8091    (8054)
8. Dave Steen (Canada) ..............................8047    (8034)

# No. 12 -- Olympic Men's 200, Atlanta 1996:
# Johnson crushes Fredericks

I have a hard time considering a blow-out a great competition. But when the guy who was blown out is Frank Fredericks, and he runs 19.68 for a half-lap, just two-hundredths slower than the world record broken a few moments earlier, then I have to reconsider.

We all know now that Michael Johnson can sandbag with the best of them. "Conserve energy," however, is the term I should use to avoid flames. And he had plenty of reason to conserve, as he was in the midst of a difficult double, the 200 and 400. No man had ever won both in the Olympics, though two women had.

After winning his semi in an eased-up 20.27, Johnson didn't look quite like the man who had run a world-record 19.66 at the Olympic Trials. Then Fredericks, who had beaten Johnson a month earlier, blasted 19.98 in his semi. The buzz indicated Johnson might have a race on his hands.

In the final, Johnson got out well, while Fredericks lagged. Both ran hot on the turn. Johnson passed 100 in 10.12, Fredericks in 10.14. Then Johnson found a gear that the rest of humanity has only dreamed about. He tore away from Fredericks as if the Namibian were jogging. He flashed across the finish with a scream while Fredericks came in nearly five meters behind.

The time, 19.32, could last for decades as the world record. Fredericks, 19.68 in second, and Ato Boldon, 19.80 in third, were stunned. Said Boldon, "If someone had told me Michael would run 19.32, I wouldn't have shown up."

## FINAL RESULTS (8/1)
1. Michael Johnson (USA) .................... 19.32   world record
2. Frank Fredericks (Namibia) ............. 19.68
3. Ato Bolden (Trinidad) ........................ 19.80
4. Obadele Thompson (Barbados) .......... 20.14
5. Jeff Williams (USA) ............................ 20.17
6. Ivan Garcia (Cuba) ............................ 20.21
7. Patrick Stevens (Belgium) ................. 20.27
8. Mike Marsh (USA) .............................. 20.48

# No. 11 -- Dream Mile, MLK Invitational, Philadelphia 1971: Liquori vs. Ryun

The anticipation of the match race between up-and-coming Marty Liquori and come-backing Jim Ryun captured the attention of the entire sports world. Wrote Bob Hersh in *Track and Field News*, "The build-up was probably the greatest for any single footrace since the historic 'Miracle Mile' at Vancouver in 1954."

With no pacesetter in the race, Ryun may have been favored on the cold, wet day. He could kick like no one else on earth, and he had run much faster than Villanova's Liquori (3:51.1 to 3:57.2). The race went out slowly, with both big names hitting the 440 in the middle of the pack, slower than 61 seconds. Ryun took over at halfway (2:03.3).

After the next turn, Liquori moved decisively. He passed the world record holder and led him through a lap in 56.7. The two rivals dug deeper for the last lap. Where many expected Ryun to sprint past in the last 200, Liquori tenaciously hung on and would not surrender the lead. At the finish, the challenger prevailed as both clocked 3:54.6.

Liquori downplayed his win over the legendary Ryun, saying, "It's early in the season. In the next six weeks, he'll do a lot of speed work. He should be a different runner in the last 220 yards than he was today."

Ryun told Bob Hersh, "It's only a year and two days since I began running again, so it's not too bad progress. It was such a great race, a fast race, that I can't be unhappy. The only thing I would have liked to have seen different was me in front at the tape."

## FINAL RESULTS (5/16)
1. Marty Liquori (Villanova) ............... 3:54.6
2. Jim Ryun (Oregon TC) .................... 3:54.6
3. Byron Dyce (Jamaica) .................... 3:59.6
4. Reggie McAfee (Brevard) ................ 4:00.0
5. Keith Colburn (Harvard) ................ 4:01.1
6. Mike Mosser (West Virginia) ........... 4:02.7
7. Joe Savage (Manhattan) ................. nt

# No. 10 -- Olympic Men's 10,000, Melbourne 1956: Kuts vs. Pirie

Soviet star Vladimir Kuts didn't just defeat his opposition in the 10,000; he destroyed it. He opened with a scorching 61.2 lap, and before long had eliminated all his rivals with the exception of Britain's Gordon Pirie, the world record holder in the 5,000. Kuts ripped through halfway in 14:07 (the Olympic record was 14:06.6) as Pirie struggled to remain in the game.

Every time Pirie caught up, Kuts would unleash another surge, or he would move to the second or third lane, urging the Briton to pass him. Not until 8K did Pirie take the bait. Within a lap, Kuts had flown by him at top speed, crushing him psychologically. Pirie faded to eighth place, more than a minute behind Kuts' winning 28:45.6, an Olympic record.

Five days later, Kuts dominated the 5,000-meter field to win in an Olympic-record 13:39.6. This time, a recovered (and wiser) Pirie hung on for the silver medal.

## FINAL RESULTS (11/25)
1. Vladimir Kuts (Soviet Union) ................ 28:45.6
2. József Kovács (Hungary) ........................ 28:52.4
3. Allan Lawrence (Australia) .................... 28:53.6
4. Zdzislaw Krzyszkowiak (Poland) ........... 29:05.0
5. Kenneth Norris (Australia) .................... 29:21.6
6. Ivan Chernyavskiy (Soviet Union) ......... 29:31.6
7. David Power (Australia) ........................ 29:49.6
8. Gordon Pirie (Great Britain) ................. 30:00.6

# No. 9 -- Empire Games Men's Mile, Vancouver 1954: Bannister vs. Landy

First Britain's Roger Bannister earned immortality by breaking the four-minute mile with his time of 3:59.4. Six weeks later, Australian rival John Landy broke that mark with a 3:58.0, in another rabbited attempt.

The first true race under four minutes came when the two met at summer's end in the forerunner of the Commonwealth Games. Hype ran high: The race earned the label, "the Miracle Mile." The bookies tabbed Landy as the favorite with 4-to-1 odds.

On the first lap, two English runners boxed Landy in, giving rise to the suspicion of team tactics. One of the Brits, however, soon lost a shoe, and Landy burst into the lead on the second turn. He hit the quarter in 58.2, with Bannister lagging in fifth. At the half, Landy clocked 1:58.2, and still had seven yards on Bannister. A 59.3 third lap brought Bannister within two yards of Landy, who led at 2:58.4.

Landy rightfully feared Bannister's kick, and sprinted from the bell as if his life depended on it. Bannister struggled to stay close, and on the final straightaway, finally made his move. As Landy looked over his left shoulder to see where he was, Bannister pulled even and passed on the right.

The Briton crossed victorious in 3:58.8 to Landy's 3:59.6. So the pace had been so exhausting that neither man, despite the importance and closeness of the contest, could break 30 seconds for the final half-lap. In his autobiography, Bannister wrote of the race, "John Landy had shown me what a race could really be at its greatest."

## FINAL RESULTS (8/7)
1. Roger Bannister (Great Britain) ........ 3:58.8
2. John Landy (Australia) ...................... 3:59.6
3. Rich Ferguson (Canada) .................... 4:07.8
4. Victor Milligan (Great Britain) .......... 4:05.0
5. Murray Halberg (New Zealand) ......... 4:07.2
6. Ian Boyd (Great Britain) ................... 4:07.2
7. Bill Baillie (New Zealand) ................. 4:11.0

# No. 8 — Olympic Men's Discus, Tokyo 1964: Oerter vs. Danek

Few figured that Al Oerter could win a third straight discus gold. Not only had he been troubled by a bad cervical disc, but doctors told him not to compete because of torn cartilage in his rib cage.

Oerter whipped an Olympic-record toss of 198 feet, 7 (60.54) inches in the qualifying round, causing the pundits to redraw their formcharts. In the final, however, the mighty Kansan struggled. After four rounds, Oerter was only in fourth place. Ludvik Danek, the world record holder from Czechoslovakia, led at 198-7 (60.52). Oerter was more than seven feet behind at 191-5 (58.34), throwing hurt. He said, "It felt like someone was trying to tear out my ribs."

Then, in a performance that defined what performing under pressure is all about, Oerter hurled the discus out to 200-1 (61.00), another Olympic record. He became the second man in history to win three consecutive golds in Olympic track and field.

## FINAL RESULTS (10/15)

1. Al Oerter (USA) .................................. 61.00        200-1
*(57.65/189-1, 58.34/191-5, 55.11/180-9, 54.37/178-4, 61.00/200-1, foul)*
2. Ludvik Danek (Czechoslovakia).......... 60.52        198-7
*(59.73/195-11, 58.83/193-0, foul, 60.52/198-7, 58.38/191-6, 57.17/187-6)*
3. Dave Weill (USA)............................... 59.49        195-2
4. Jay Silvester (USA)............................ 59.09        193-10
5. Jozsef Szecsenyi (Hungary) ................ 57.23        187-9
6. Zenon Begier (Poland)........................ 57.06        187-2
7. Edmund Piatkowski (Poland) ............. 55.81        183-1
8. Vladimir Trusenev (Soviet Union) ...... 54.78        179-9

# No. 7 -- AAU Indoor Men's 600 Yards, New York 1970: McGrady vs. Evans

The finest indoor race of all time went to a man who barely earned a footnote for his accomplishments outdoors. Martin McGrady, a national class quarter miler, turned into a superhuman on the boards. In seven races leading up to the AAU national championships, he piled up seven victories and three world records.

With over 15,000 fans watching in Madison Square Garden, McGrady lined up in lane 2 against Olympic 400 champion Lee Evans (lane 4) to contest the now-defunct 600-yard distance. McGrady took off like a shot, showing no signs of fatigue from his 1:10.9 heat earlier in the night: "I decided to be a rabbit for once." By the end of the first straightaway, he had a five-yard lead on Evans.

McGrady hit 440 yards in 48.6 as observers called the pace "suicidal." He later told *Track & Field News*, "Brooks Johnson and I decided that I would run the first quarter as if that was the whole race and then go with what I had left from there. I knew Lee had the strength to be somewhere near but I hoped to discourage him with a fast quarter."

All eyes watched for Evans to begin his late-race drive. At one point, it looked like he might summon the strength to run McGrady down. But McGrady found another gear, and steamed across the line in 1:07.6, crushing his old mark of 1:08.5. Evans, at 1:08.0, also bettered the old record: " "I lost the race on the turns," Evans said. "I just can't stay inside. I go wide on every turn. At the end I knew I was catching him but I just ran out of straightaway."

Said McGrady, "This is the first race in a long time that has left me with hardly anything at the end." Indeed, he never again approached that time in his career. It wasn't until Mark Everett ran 1:07.53 in 1992 that the record, which gained luster with each passing year, finally fell. IAAF council member Bob Hersh, who reported on the race that day, still raves about McGrady's run as the greatest in indoor history.

## FINAL RESULTS (2/27)

1. Martin McGrady (Sports International) ..........1:07.6  world record
2. Lee Evans (unattached)..................................1:08.0
3. Pete Schuder (Philadelphia Pioneer Club).......1:10.6
4. Ron Whitney (Striders)..................................1:10.9

# No. 6 -- Olympic Men's 100 meters, Seoul 1988: Johnson vs. Lewis

The reviled Ben Johnson's infamous Olympic final remains one of the most exciting races ever seen by those who witnessed it first-hand. The fiercest of rivals, Johnson and Carl Lewis couldn't have stood in greater contrast: Johnson was short, powerful, and bouncing with overabundant energy, while the taller, thinner Lewis stood calmly before the start.

Johnson's start had to be the greatest in history. He exploded from the blocks, putting Lewis into a hole from which he could never recover. By 20 meters, Johnson led by 0.07. At halfway, he had more than a tenth of a second. Like an enraged animal finally set free, the Canadian ferociously clawed his way to the finish. Lewis mounted his classic finishing drive, but he let up in the final strides when he saw how futile his efforts were. "I knew I couldn't get him," he later wrote. His coach, Tom Tellez, said, "He could have run a faster time if he'd forgotten about Ben and run his own race. If you're looking at someone else, you're not really running your own race."

Johnson crossed in 9.79, breaking his old world record of 9.83. Lewis crossed in 9.92. A day later, Johnson was disqualified, testing positive for the steroid stanolozol. A year later, both of Johnson's world records were erased, and record recognition went to Lewis and his 9.92.

What is history to do with the notion of revised results? The revision, not seen before or since at this level, came about as a result of massive public and political pressure. Never before had the sport been so embarrassed in its ultimate showcase; the cost in lost sponsorships, to this day, is immeasurable. Yet the race happened; Johnson demolished Lewis in a contest that was as highly anticipated and thrilling -- at the time -- as any in history. And only the stat types seem to have noticed that, while only Johnson faced eternal public damnation, half of the field that day was later implicated in various doping scandals.

## FINAL RESULTS (9/24)

DQ. Ben Johnson (Canada)...................... 9.79
1. Carl Lewis (USA)................................. 9.92  world record
2. Linford Christie (Great Britain) .......... 9.97
3. Calvin Smith (USA)............................. 9.99
4. Dennis Mitchell (USA)......................... 10.04
5. Robson da Silva (Brazil)...................... 10.11
6. Desai Williams (Canada) ..................... 10.11
7. Raymond Stewart (Jamaica)................. 12.26

# No. 5 — World Championships Men's 400 Hurdles, Rome 1987: Moses over Harris & Schmid

Edwin Moses, in lane three, may have lost his win streak earlier in the year to Danny Harris, but he still ruled supreme over the long hurdles. Harris stood in lane five. Between the two stood West German Harald Schmid, the European record holder, and the last man to beat Moses before his win streak started 10 years earlier.

Moses used the inside lane to his advantage, rocketing out at a hellacious pace while his opponents wondered where he was. By the fifth hurdle, it became apparent to all that Moses had a two-meter lead over Harris and Schmid. Instead of pulling away, however, it was all the king could do to hold on.

At the final hurdle, the exhausted Moses led by a mere three feet. Harris stumbled and lost ground, while Schmid moved into second. All three sprinted hard, with Harris moving fastest. All three leaned at the same time. Observers could not tell who had won. Moses started on his victory lap ("perhaps from habit alone" observed Track and Field News). Harris and Schmid waited for the verdict.

Moses claimed the gold in 47.46, while Harris and Schmid both timed 47.48. No one had ever run faster for second or third place -- or fourth, fifth, sixth, seventh and eighth, for that matter. All hailed it the greatest hurdle race ever.

## FINAL RESULTS (9/1)
1. Edwin Moses (USA) ............................ 47.46
2. Danny Harris (USA) .......................... 47.48
3. Harald Schmid (West Germany) ........ 47.48
4. Sven Nylander (Sweden) ................... 48.37
5. Amadou Dia Bá (Senegal) ................. 48.37
6. Henry Amike (Nigeria) ...................... 48.63
7. Kriss Akabusi (Great Britain) .......... 48.74
8. José Alonso (Spain) ........................... 49.46

# No. 4 -- Olympic Men's Steeplechase, Montreal 1976: Garderud vs. Malinowski

Expectations ran high for this event, and only got higher when five men ran faster than the Olympic record in the heats.

In the final, Spain's Antonio Campos went out hard, but soon, favored Bronislaw Malinowski took over. The Pole was followed closely by Sweden's world record holder, Anders Garderud, East Germany's Frank Baumgartl, and Finland's Tapio Kantanen. At 2,000m (5:29.1), the foursome still hovered near world-record pace.

Garderud waited until the last 300 to make his move. He dashed past Malinowski, with Baumgartl close behind. The two were even at the last water jump, but Garderud, a better hurdler, gained a step there. Still, it looked to many as if the East German had enough momentum to catch Garderud at the last hurdle. Instead, Baumgartl chopped his step and slammed into the immovable barrier with his trail leg.

The crowd gasped as Baumgartl hit the ground hard. Malinowski hurdled over him, but Baumgartl still rose to his feet and desperately raced to the finish to grab the bronze medal in a personal-best 8:10.4. The two men who had beaten him had both slipped under the old world record: Garderud 8:08.0, Malinowski 8:09.2.

Said Baumgartl, "I remembered that when this happened to Lasse Viren... in Munich, Lasse got up and won. It was just instinct to continue, and I don't even want to speculate on whether or not I would have won."

Garderud's performance was the last steeplechase record to belong to a non-Kenyan. The depth of the race, when compared to today's European times, shows just how clearly non-Africans have conceded the event to the Kenyans.

## FINAL RESULTS (7/28)

1. Anders Gärderud (Sweden)......................8:08.0  world record
2. Bronislaw Malinowski (Poland)..............8:09.2    (8:09.11)
3. Frank Baumgartl (East Germany)..........8:10.4    (8:10.36)
4. Tapio Kantanen (Finland) ......................8:12.6    (8:12.60)
5. Michael Karst (West Germany) ..............8:20.2    (8:20.14)
6. Euan Robertson (New Zealand) ..............8:21.2    (8:21.08)
7. Dan Glans (Sweden) ...............................8:21.6    (8:21.53)
8. Antonio Campos (Spain) ........................8:22.8    (8:22.65)

# No. 3 -- World Championships Women's 1,500, Helsinki 1983: Decker over the Soviets

Mary Decker would never be better. The woman whom American fans either love or hate, Decker would not be denied in the summer of 1983. At the first World Championships, she faced the Soviets at their best. First, she stunned them by leading the 3,000 meters from start to finish, winning with a powerful kick that few expected she would have left.

Four days later came the 1,500. She faced three Soviets who had broken four minutes, led by Zamara Zaitseva (3:56.14), who false-started out of nervousness. Once the race got off in earnest, Decker hesitated before taking the lead. She hit 400 in 64.1, then slowed for a 2:11.0 at 800.

The pace favored kickers, and the Soviets looked very dangerous. Decker ran 65.7 for her third lap, then opened up some daylight on the backstretch. Zaitseva stayed close, and Yekaterina Podkopayeva tried to catch them. On the final turn, Zaitseva took the lead as Decker had to cut short her stride.

Decker entered the homestretch two meters behind, feeling like she had lost her momentum. With 60 meters left, she regrouped and charged. "I didn't want to feel that I cheated myself by not trying hard enough," she said. With 10 meters left, she came alongside Zaitseva. The Russian dived early and fell five meters from the line. Decker crossed victorious in 4:00.90 for her second gold as Zaitseva slid across in 4:01.19. It was the first-ever gold in a World or Olympic distance race for an American woman.

## FINAL RESULTS (8/14)
1. Mary Decker (USA) .................................. 4:00.90
2. Zamira Zaytseva (Soviet Union) ............... 4:01.19
3. Yekaterina Podkopayeva (Soviet Union) ... 4:02.25
4. Ravilya Agletdinova (Soviet Union) .......... 4:02.67
5. Wendy Sly (Great Britain) ........................ 4:04.14
6. Doina Melinte (Romania) .......................... 4:04.42
7. Gabriella Dorio (Italy) ............................. 4:04.73
8. Brit McRoberts (Canada) .......................... 4:05.73

# No. 2 -- World Championships Men's Long Jump, Tokyo 1991: Powell vs. Lewis

Bob Beamon's historic 29-2½ long jump in Mexico City reigned as the world record for nearly 23 years; many had considered it to be unbreakable. Carl Lewis had come close at several points in his career, and with a 10-year, 65-meet win streak, was widely considered the only man who had a chance.

On a hot, steamy night in Tokyo, Lewis faced his toughest rival, Mike Powell. Sometimes called "Powell the Foul" by those who criticized his inconsistency on the board, Powell knew he was ready to take on Lewis. An opening leap of 25-9¼ did not detract from that confidence. Lewis came up with a solid 28-5¾. Powell edged closer with a 28-¼, then Lewis popped 28-11¾ on his third attempt, the longest jump of his career, though wind-aided.

On his fourth jump, Lewis tightened his grip on the gold with an improvement to 29-2¾, again with a wind over the allowable. Then Powell unleashed his stunner. Slower on the runway than his rival, he had a much more explosive take-off. He soared into the air to land at 29-4½. The wind reading, a legal 0.3, confirmed he had broken Beamon's record. A jubilant Powell lifted an alarmed Japanese official off the ground in a bear hug.

Lewis, with two jumps remaining, had to come through like he never had before. He had been chasing Beamon's mark all his career, and now he needed to go well beyond it just to win. His fifth jump of 29-1¼ -- against the wind -- gave him a personal best, but no gold. After Powell passed his final attempt, a nervous Lewis pulled himself together for his last try. He soared to 29-0, one of the finest jumps in history, but only the fourth farthest of the day.

## FINAL RESULTS (8/30)

1. Mike Powell (USA)............................8.95  29-4½  world record
*(7.85/25-9¼, 8.54/28-¼, 8.29/27-2½, f, 8.95/29-4½, f)*
2. Carl Lewis (USA)...............................8.91w  29-2¾w
*(8.68/28-5¾, f, 8.83/28-11¾w, 8.91/29-2¾w, 8.87/29-1¼, 8.84/29-0)*
3. Larry Myricks (USA) ..........................8.42  27-7½
4. Dietmar Haaf (Germany)....................8.22w  26-11¾w
5. Bogdan Tudor (Romania)....................8.06  26-5½
6. David Culbert (Australia) .................8.02  26-3¾
7. Giovanni Evangelisti (Italy)...............8.01  26-3½
8. Volodymyr Ochkan (Soviet Union).....7.99w  26-2¾w

# No. 1 -- Olympic Men's 10,000, Tokyo 1964: Mills Shocks the World

Conventional wisdom for most armchair coaches is that if you're the world record holder, and you don't have a kick, what you need to do to win a gold is to run as if you're going for a record. If the opposition can't keep up, then you win.

That's what sprintless Ron Clarke tried in Tokyo. Running near the front all the way on a damp track, he pushed the leaders to a world-record pace. At halfway, the leader actually was Sioux Indian Billy Mills in 14:04.6, but Clarke lurked a step behind. "I was thinking that I couldn't continue at this pace," said Mills.

In the second half the pace eased somewhat, and by the last lap, only three remained: Clarke, Mills, and Mohamed Gammoudi of Tunisia. Mills gained confidence when he saw a worried Clarke glance back. On the last curve, Mills tried to use a lapped runner to box Clarke in. The Australian tapped, then pushed Mills to escape. "I guess I pushed too hard, because he went way out," said Clarke. Gammoudi chose that moment to zip between them and take the lead, but Clarke quickly reeled him back in.

Then, with 50 meters left, Mills launched a spirited attack, stunning the world by flashing past the leaders. An astonished Clarke gave up the hunt as Mills captured the gold with an Olympic-record 28:24.4. After the finish, an official asked the U.S. Marine, "Who are you?"

Those amazed by Mills' breakthrough -- he ran approximately 35 seconds faster than his converted six-mile best -- should have been equally impressed by Gammoudi's 28:24.8 in second; he improved by an even bigger margin.

Mills later said, "At 60 yards to go, they were still ahead of me, and I couldn't hear anything except my heart pounding. And I knew I had won."

## FINAL RESULTS (10/14)
1. Billy Mills (USA) .................................................................. 28:24.4
2. Mohamed Gamoudi (Tunisia) ............................................ 28:24.8
3. Ron Clarke (Australia)...................................................... 28:25.8
4. Mamo Wolde (Ethiopia) .................................................... 28:31.8
5. Leonid Ivanov (Soviet Union) ........................................... 28:53.2
6. Kokichi Tsuburaya (Japan) ............................................... 28:59.4
7. Murray Halberg (New Zealand)......................................... 29:10.8
8. Tony Cook (Australia)....................................................... 29:15.8

# A WORD OF THANKS

Many are the fans who have suggested competitions that were
included in this series. My appreciation also goes to the
sportswriters whose work over the years has ensured a historical
record of these great competitions. A special thanks to *Track and
Field News*, without whose 63-plus years of coverage any history
of the sport would be impossible.

**Other essential sources I am thankful for:**
ATFS - *Track & Field Performances Through the Years*
Wally Donovan - *A History of Indoor Track & Field*
Richard Hymans - *The History of The U.S. Olympic Track & Field
Trials 1908-2000.*
Richard Hymans - *IAAF Progression of World Best Performances
and Official World Records.*
Mirko Jalava - Tilastopaja.com

And of course, *Track & Field News*, the Bible of the Sport;
subscription information available online at
trackandfieldnews.com